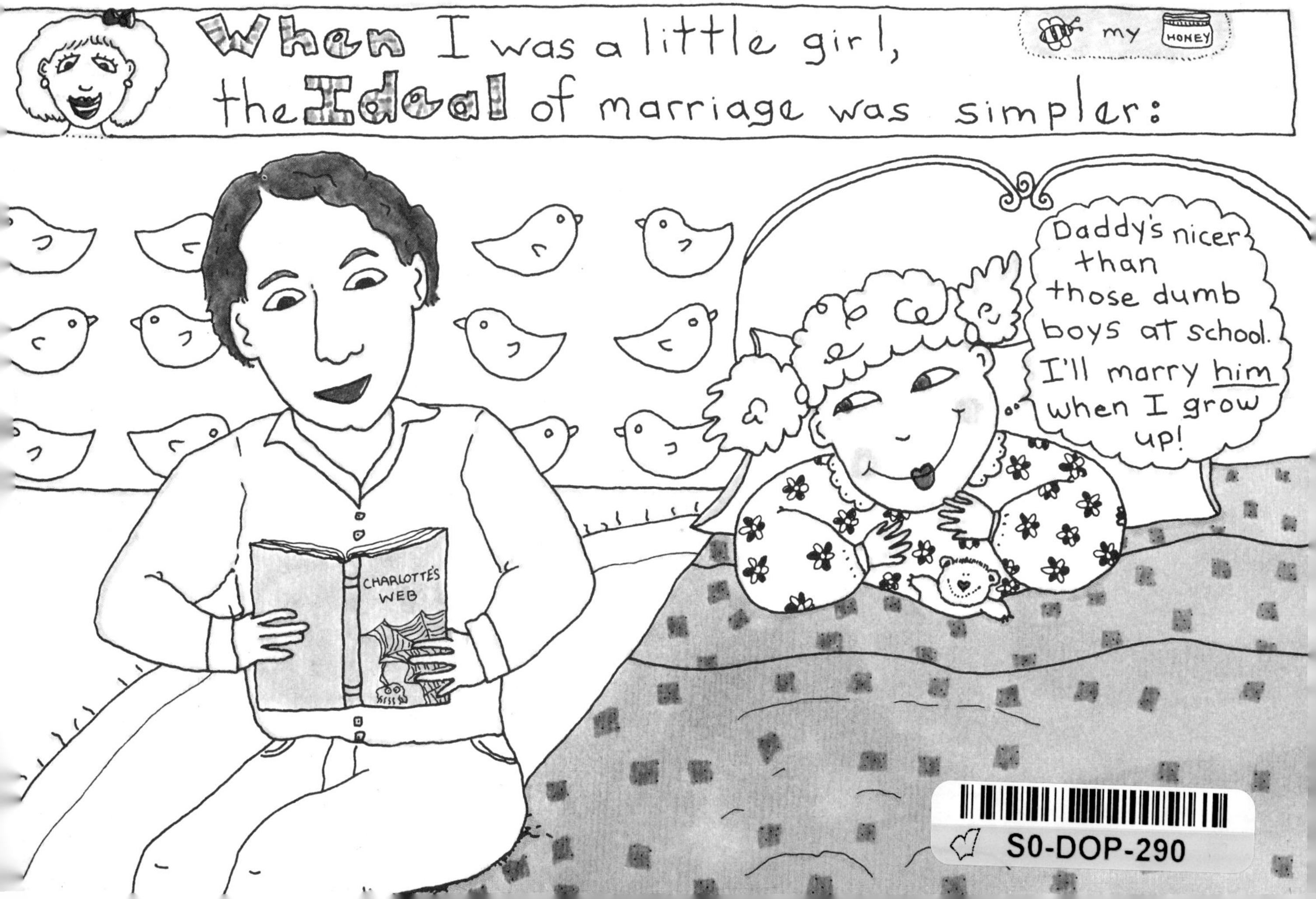
When I was a little girl,
the Ideal of marriage was simpler:
my
HONEY
Daddy's nicer than those dumb boys at school. I'll marry him when I grow up!
CHARLOTTE'S WEB

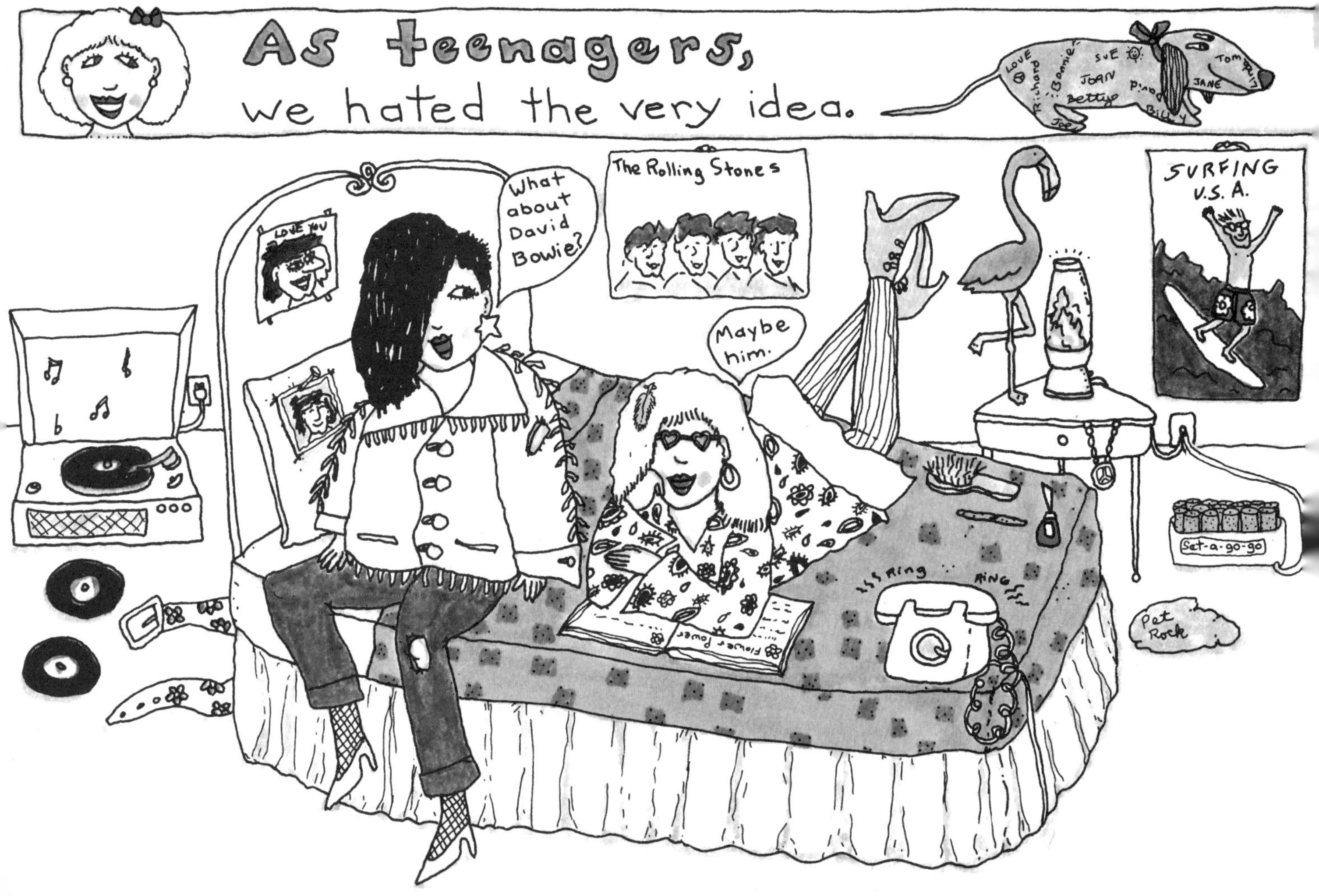
As teenagers,
we hated the very idea.
LOVE
Richard
Bonnie
SUE
JOAN
Betty
Billy
Joe
TOM
JANE
LOVE YOU
What about David Bowie?
The Rolling Stones
SURFING U.S.A.
Maybe him.
RING
RING
Flower Power
Set-a-go-go
Pet Rock

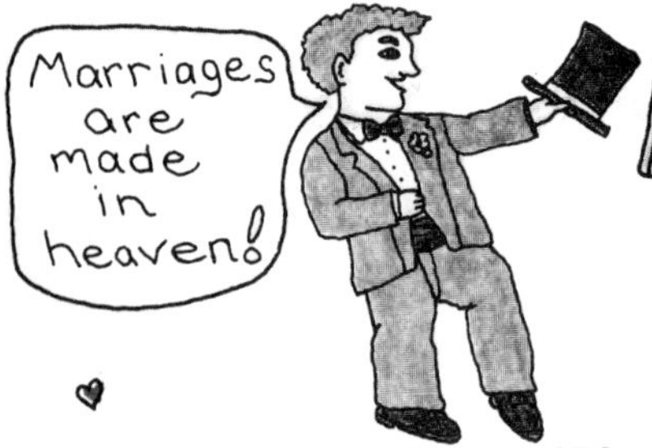
Marriages are made in heaven!

And now, you're GETTING MARRIED!

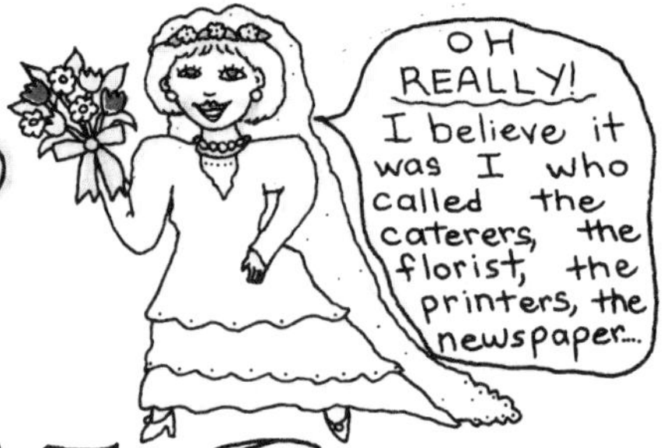
OH REALLY! I believe it was I who called the caterers, the florist, the printers, the newspaper...

A Guide for the Bride-to-Be

By Nicole Rubel

St. Martin's Press · New York

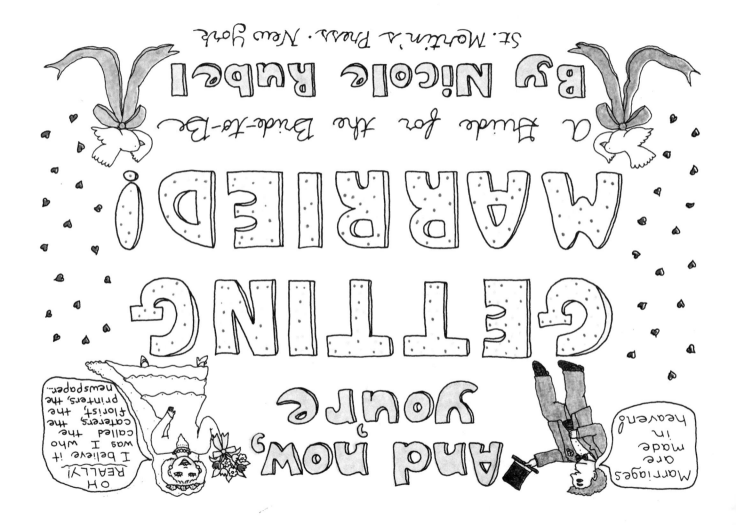

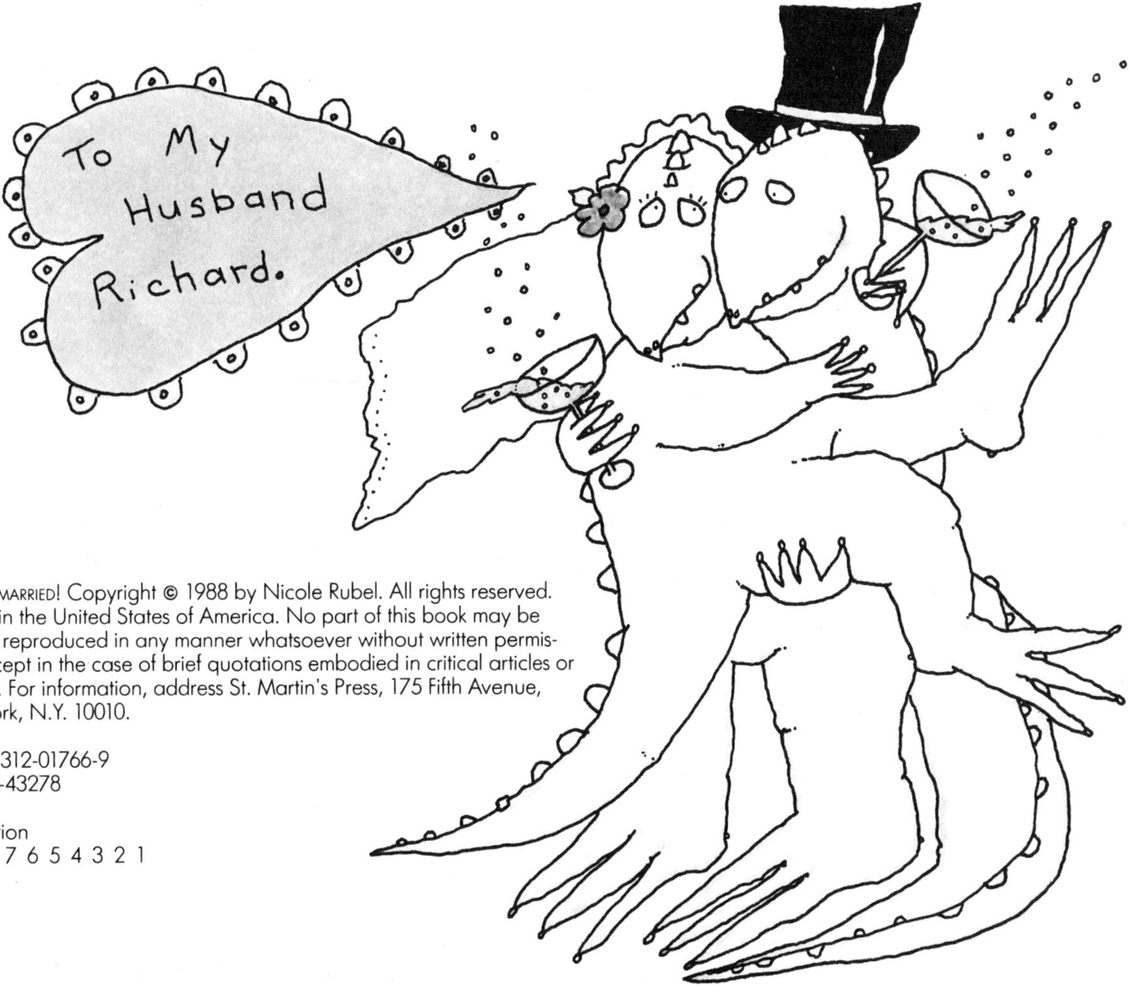
To My Husband Richard.

 For information, address St. Martin's Press, 175 Fifth Avenue, New York, N.Y. 10010.

ISBN 0-312-01766-9
LCC 87-43278

First Edition
10 9 8 7 6 5 4 3 2 1

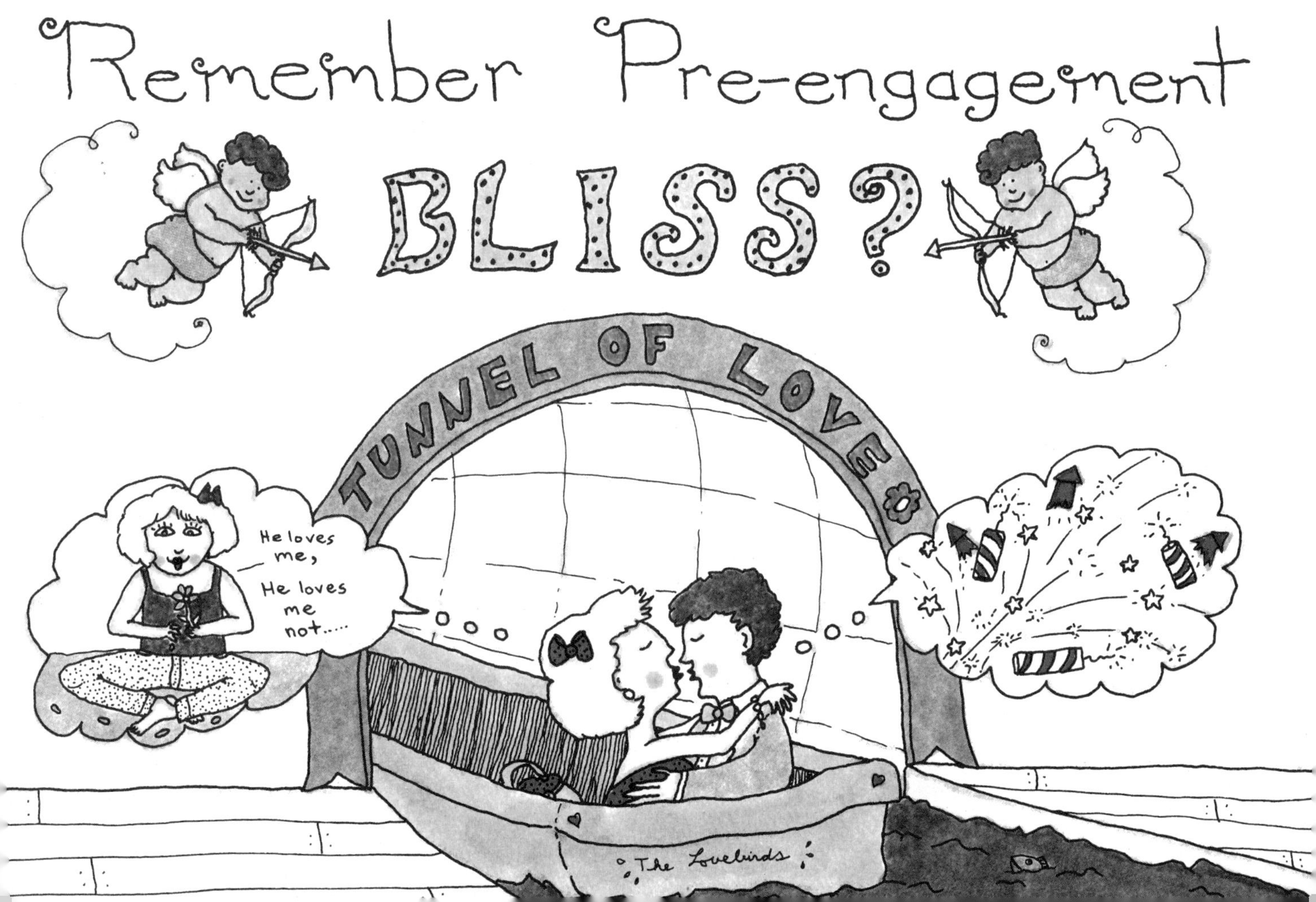
Remember Pre-engagement
BLISS?
TUNNEL OF LOVE
He loves me, He loves me not.....
The Lovebirds

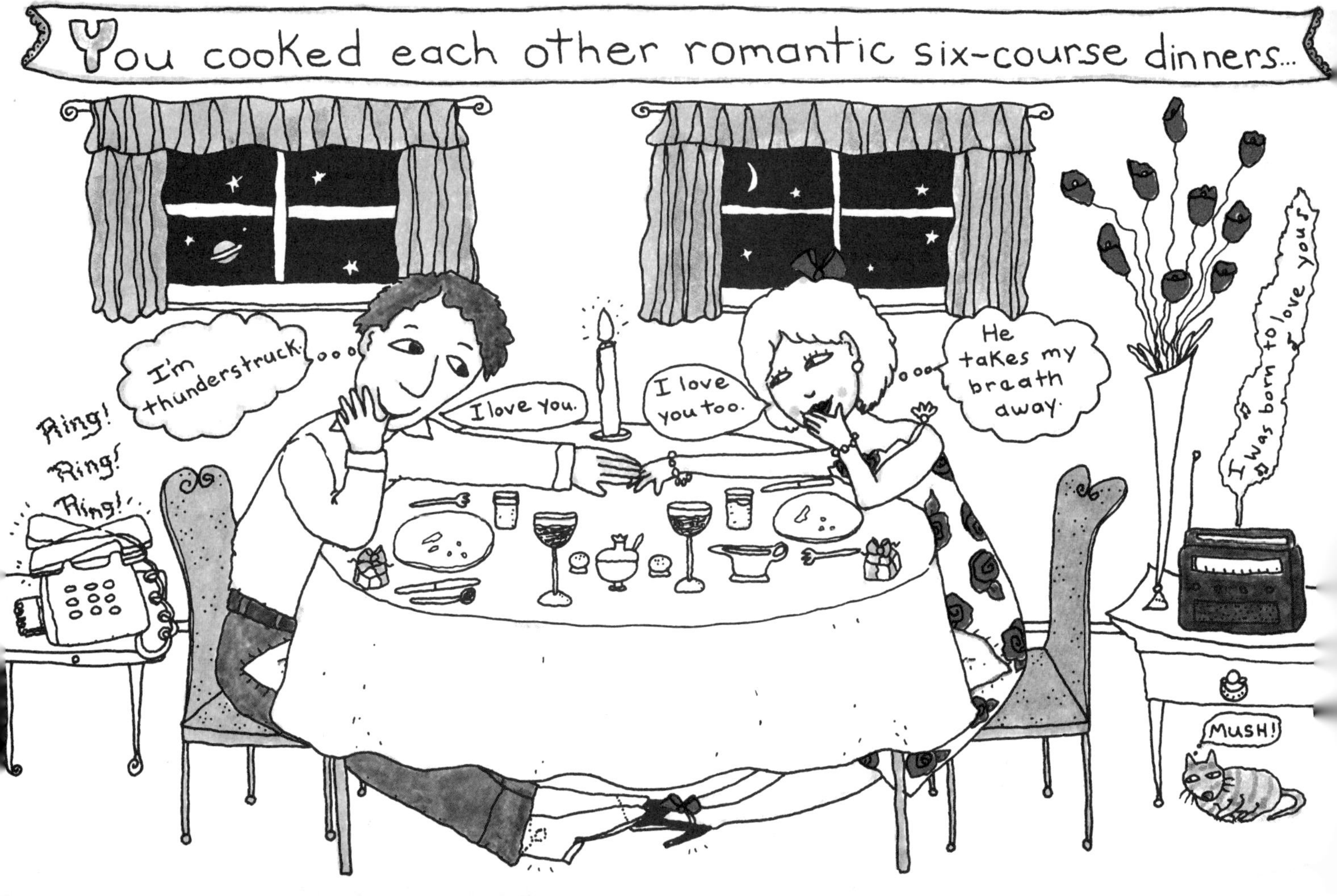
You cooked each other romantic six-course dinners...
I'm thunderstruck.
I love you.
I love you too.
He takes my breath away.
I was born to love you
Ring!
Ring!
Ring!
MUSH!

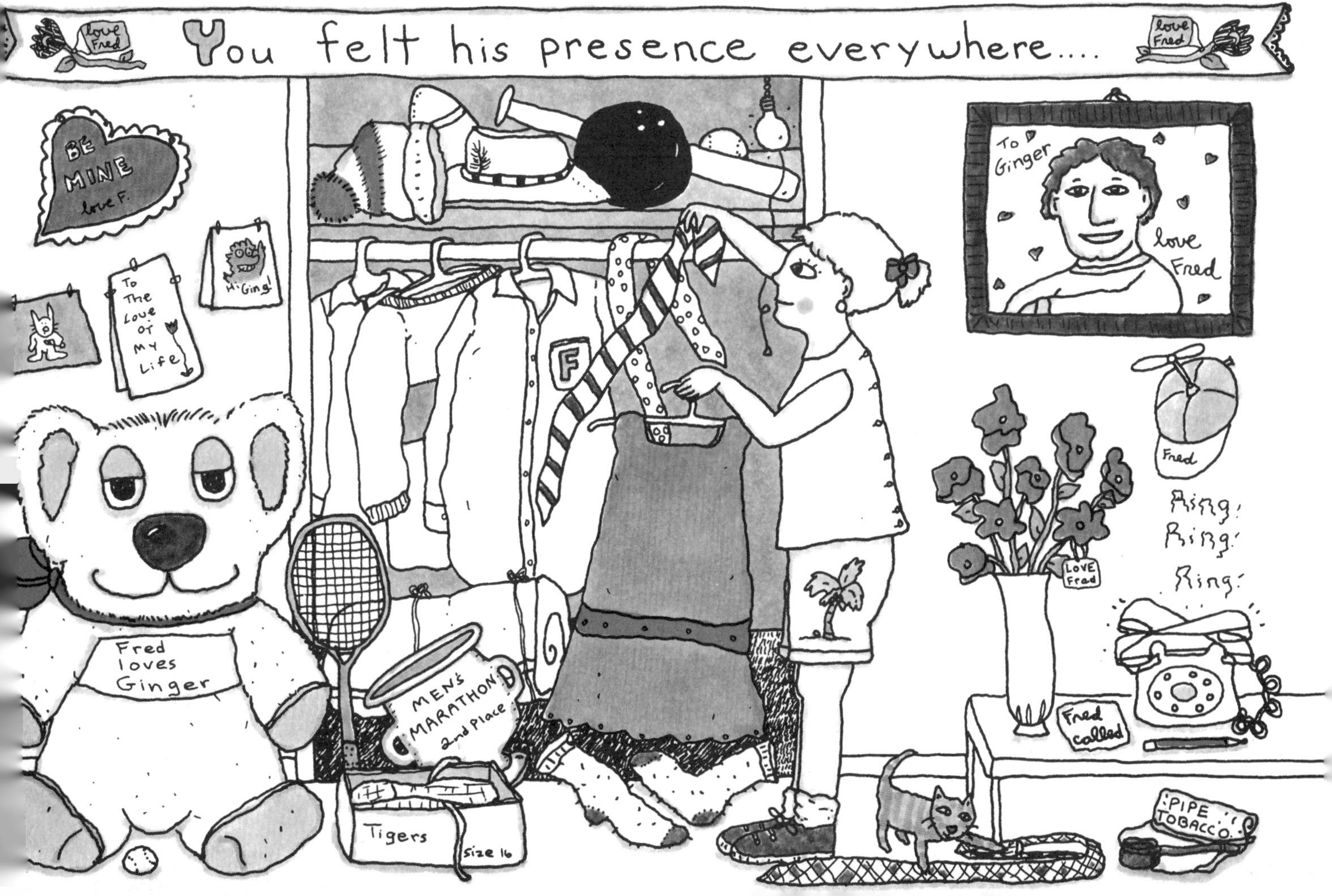
You felt his presence everywhere....
love Fred
love Fred
BE MINE love F.
Hi Ging!
To The Love of My Life
To Ginger
love Fred
F
Fred
Ring! Ring! Ring!
LOVE Fred
Fred loves Ginger
MEN'S MARATHON 2nd Place
Fred called
Tigers
size 16
PIPE TOBACCO

You Promised: We'll never fight!

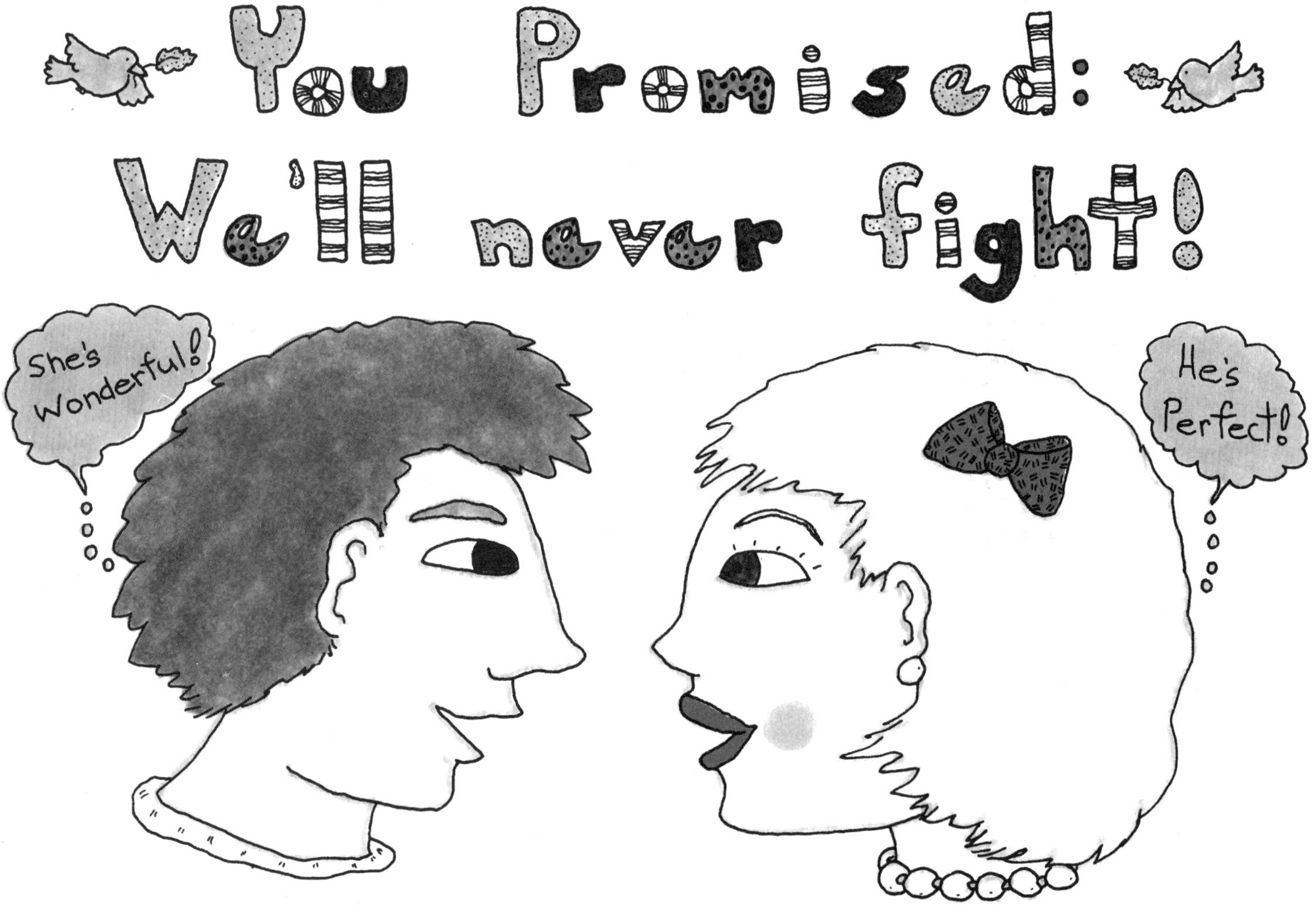
She's Wonderful!
He's Perfect!

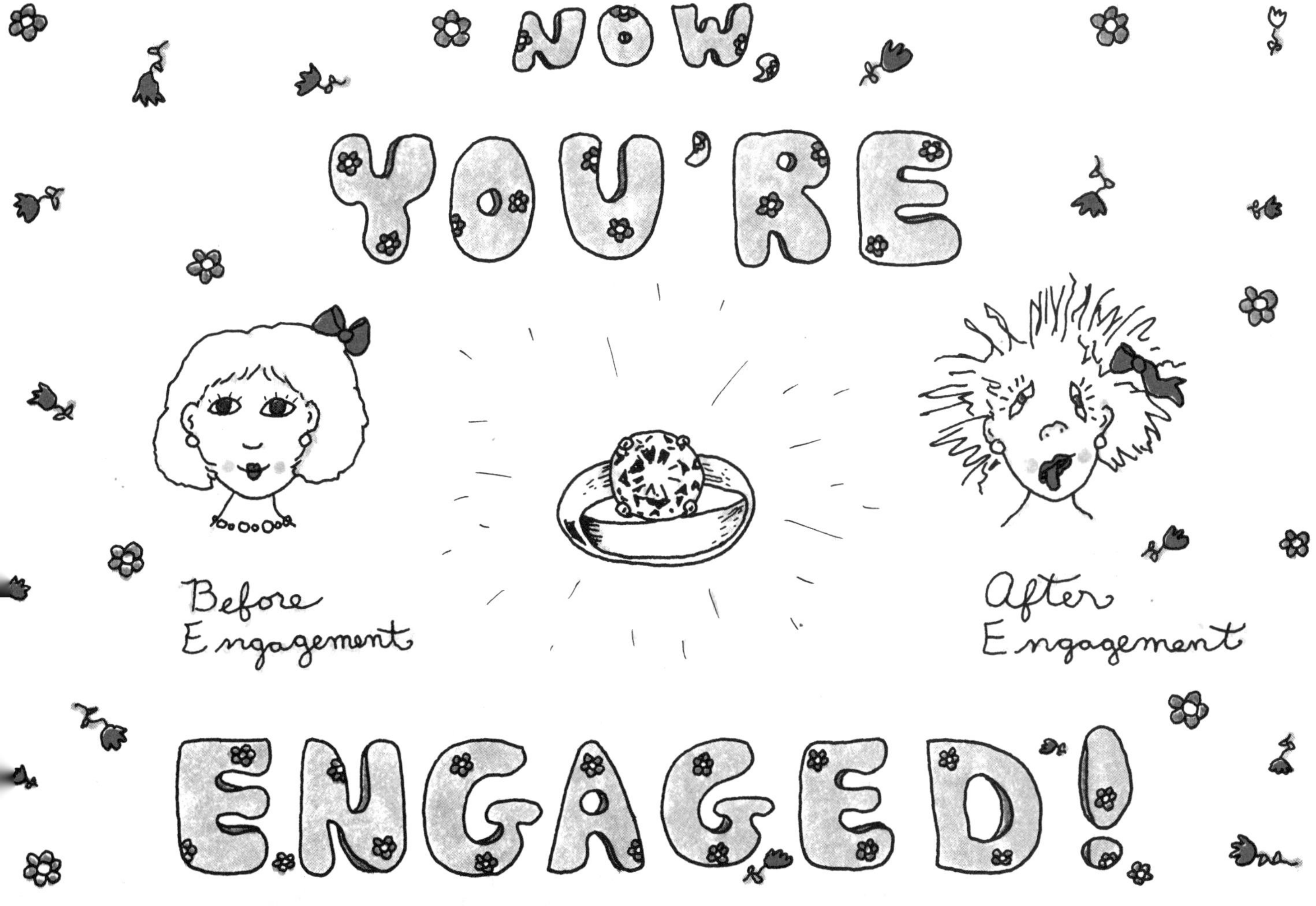
NOW, YOU'RE
Before Engagement
After Engagement
ENGAGED!

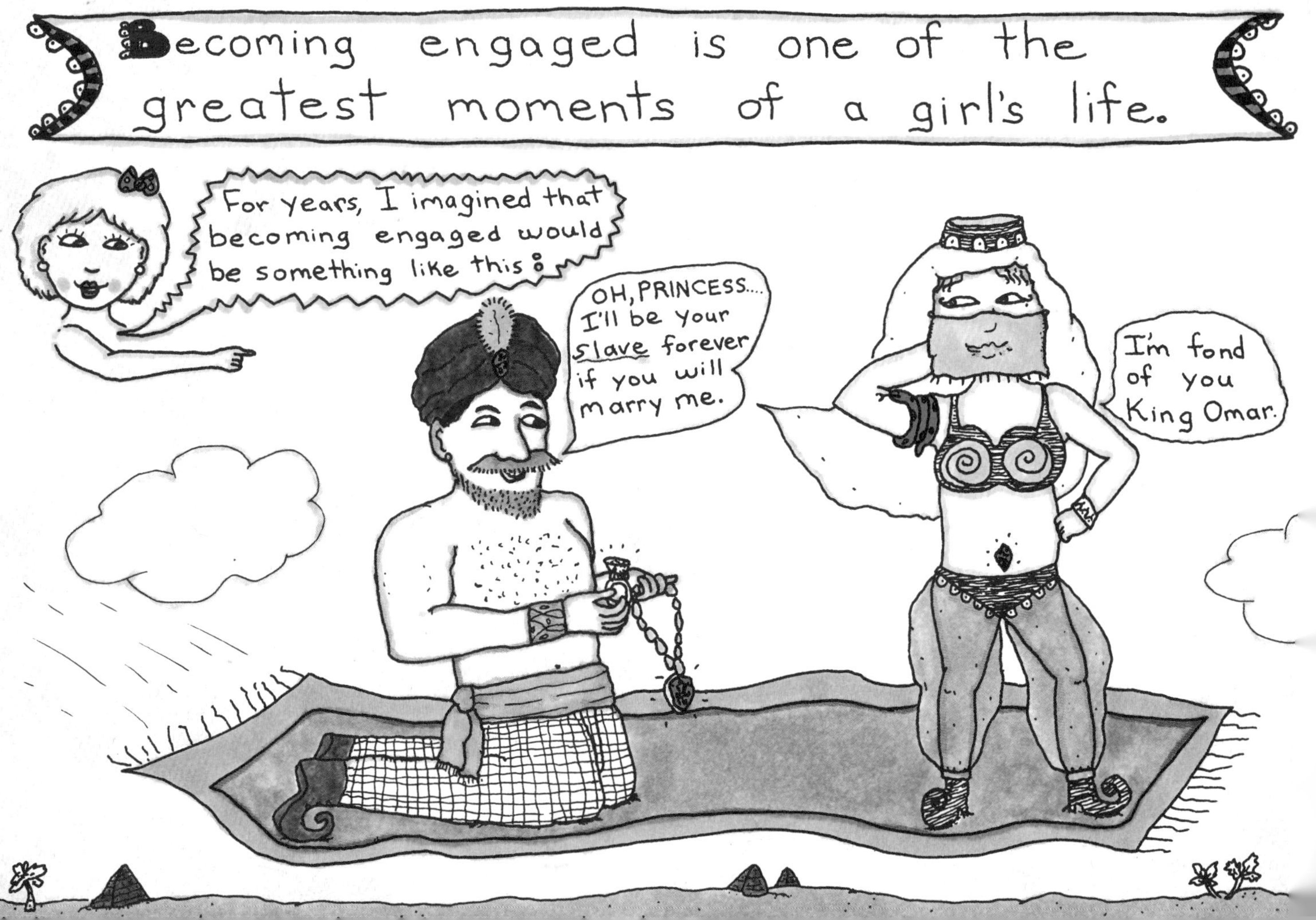
Becoming engaged is one of the greatest moments of a girl's life.
For years, I imagined that becoming engaged would be something like this:
OH, PRINCESS.... I'll be your slave forever if you will marry me.
I'm fond of you King Omar.

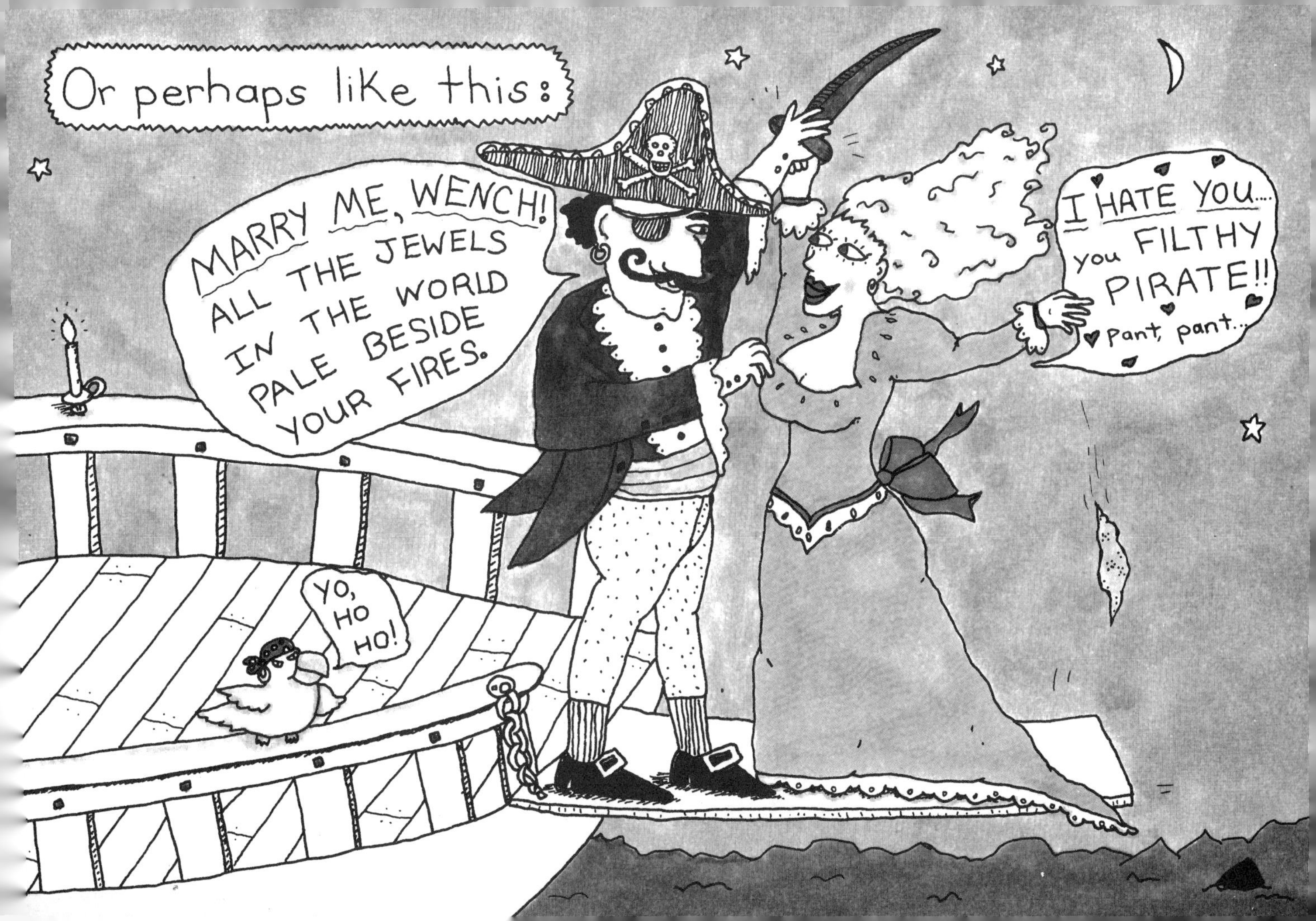
Or perhaps like this:
MARRY ME, WENCH! ALL THE JEWELS IN THE WORLD PALE BESIDE YOUR FIRES.
I HATE YOU.... you FILTHY PIRATE!! Pant, pant...
YO, HO HO!

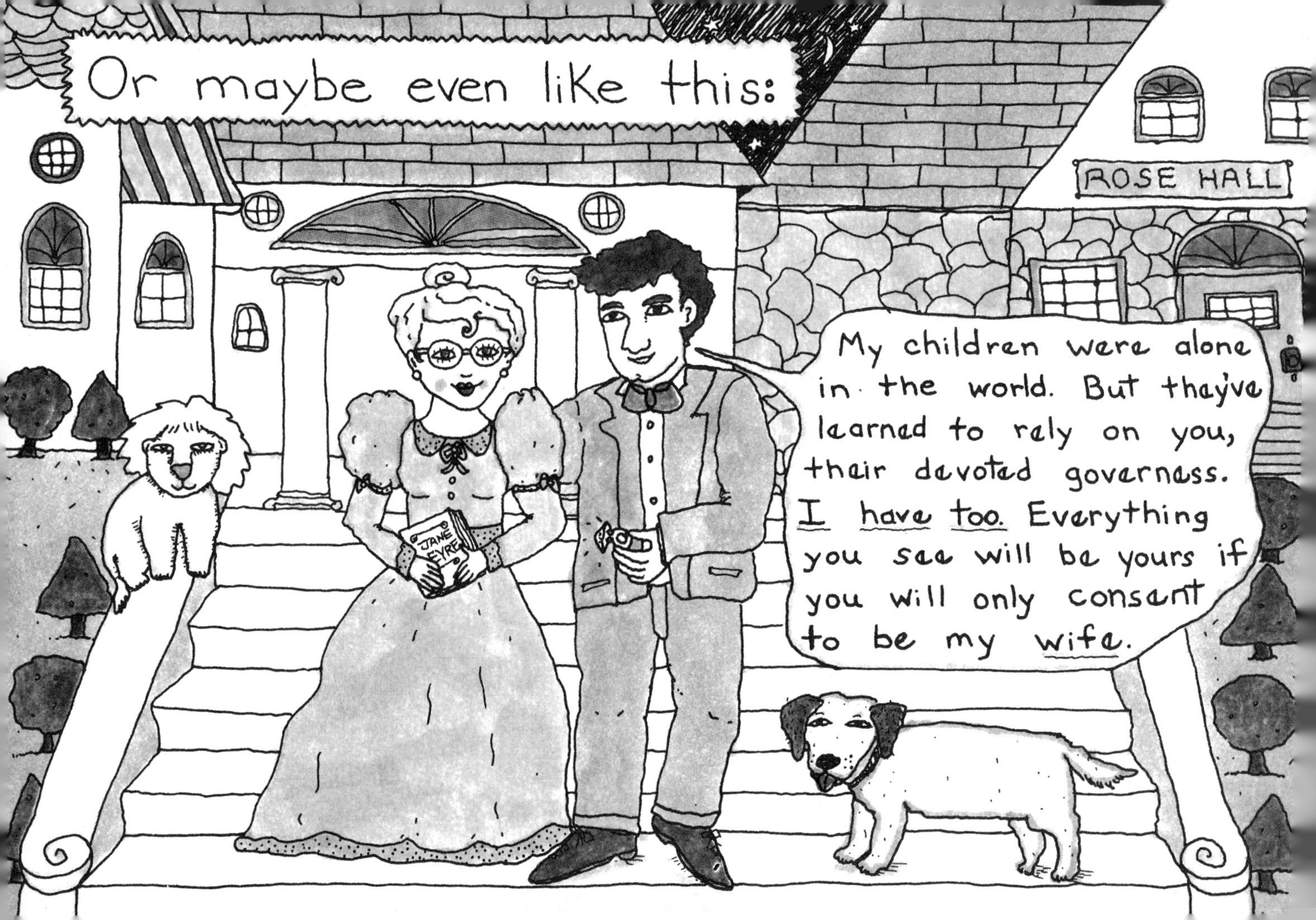
Or maybe even like this:
ROSE HALL
JANE EYRE
My children were alone in the world. But they've learned to rely on you, their devoted governess. I have too. Everything you see will be yours if you will only consent to be my wife.

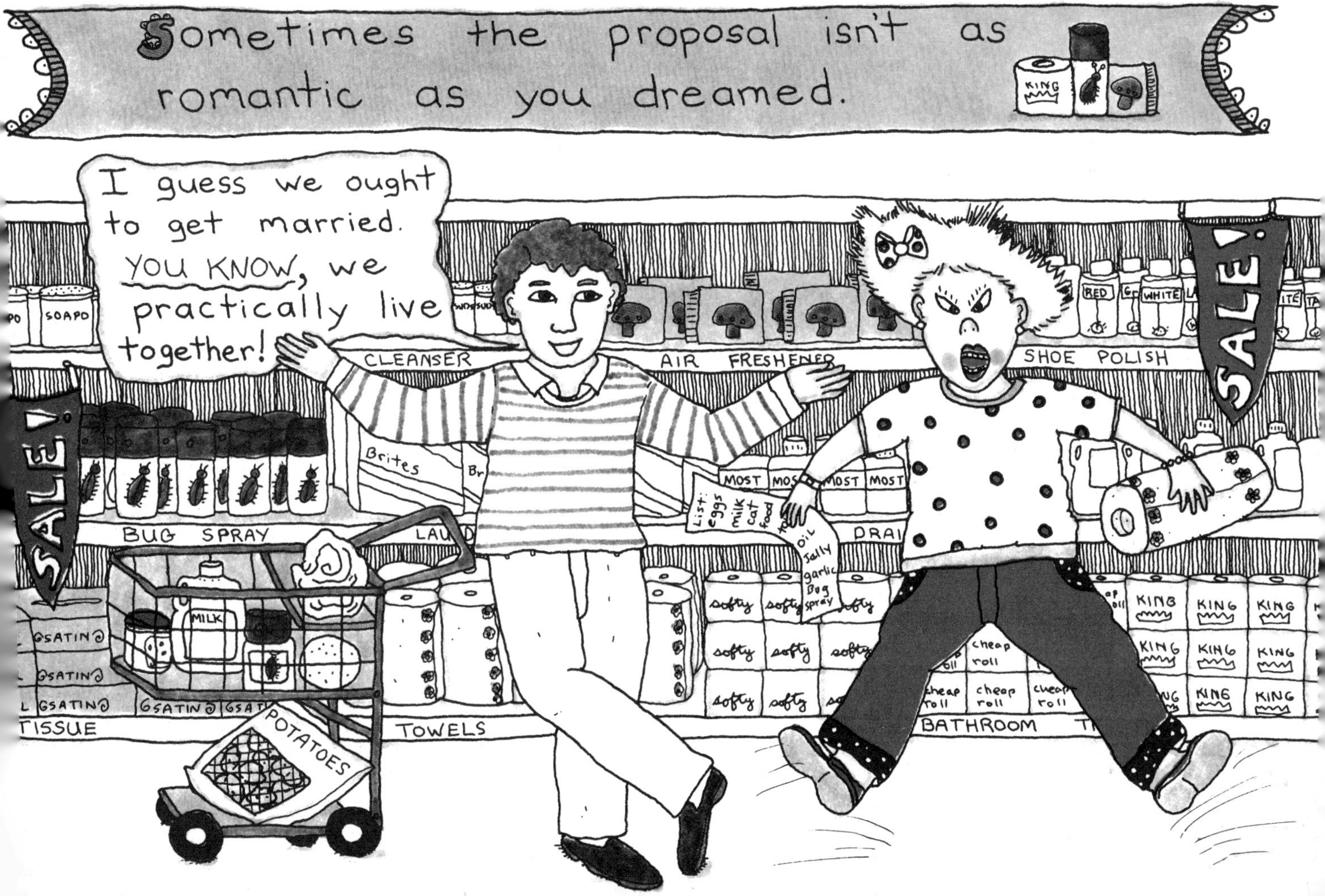
Sometimes the proposal isn't as romantic as you dreamed.
I guess we ought to get married. YOU KNOW, we practically live together!
KING
SOAPO
CLEANSER
AIR FRESHENER
SHOE POLISH
RED
WHITE
SALE!
SALE!
Brites
MOST
BUG SPRAY
List: eggs milk cat food oil Jelly garlic Bug spray
MILK
POTATOES
SATIN
softy
cheap roll
TISSUE
TOWELS
BATHROOM

The engagement is a period for pondering deeper questions.

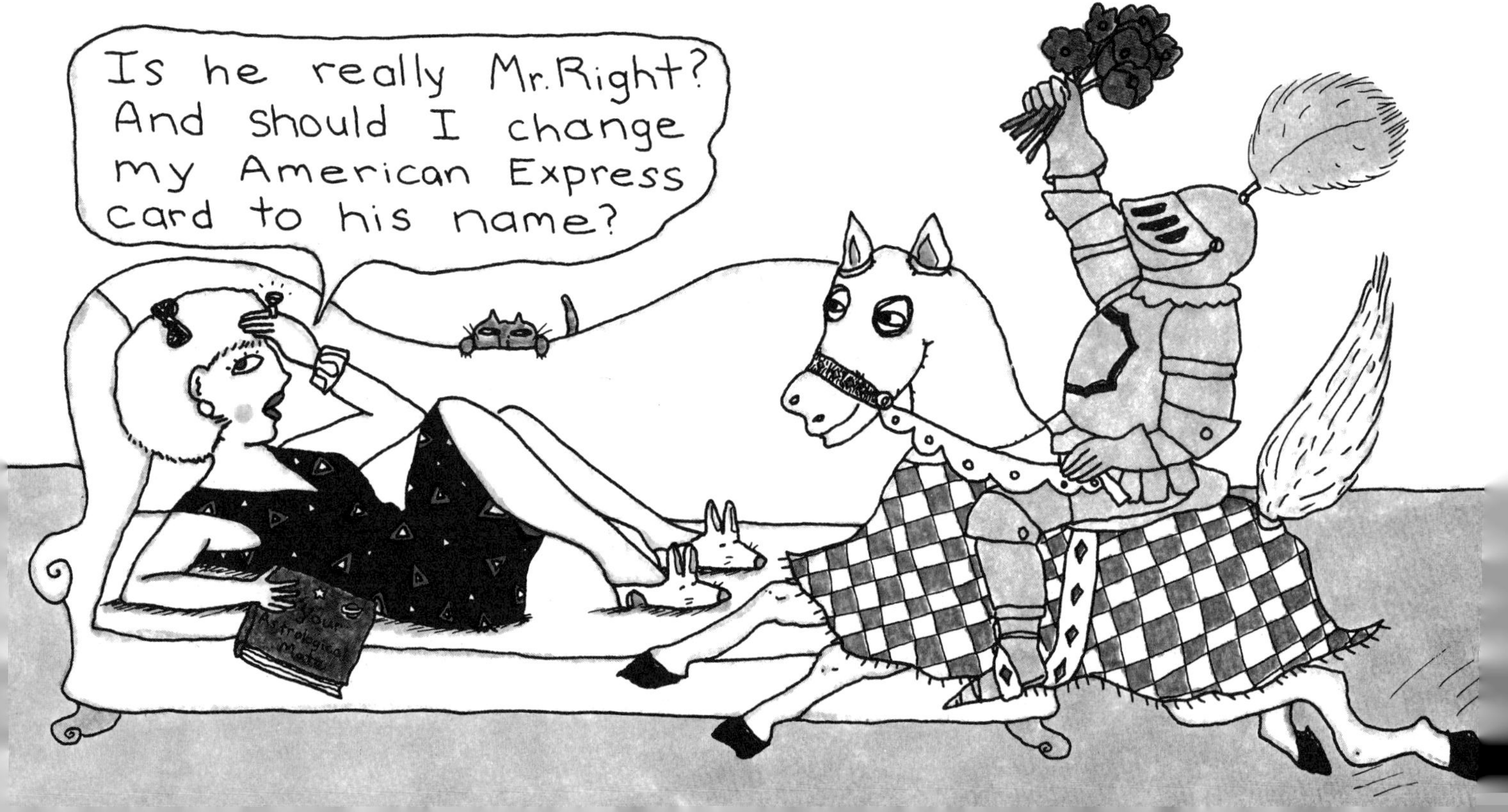
Is he really Mr. Right? And should I change my American Express card to his name?
Your Astrological Mate

And for finding out more about one another.
You'll learn that we're all creatures of habit.

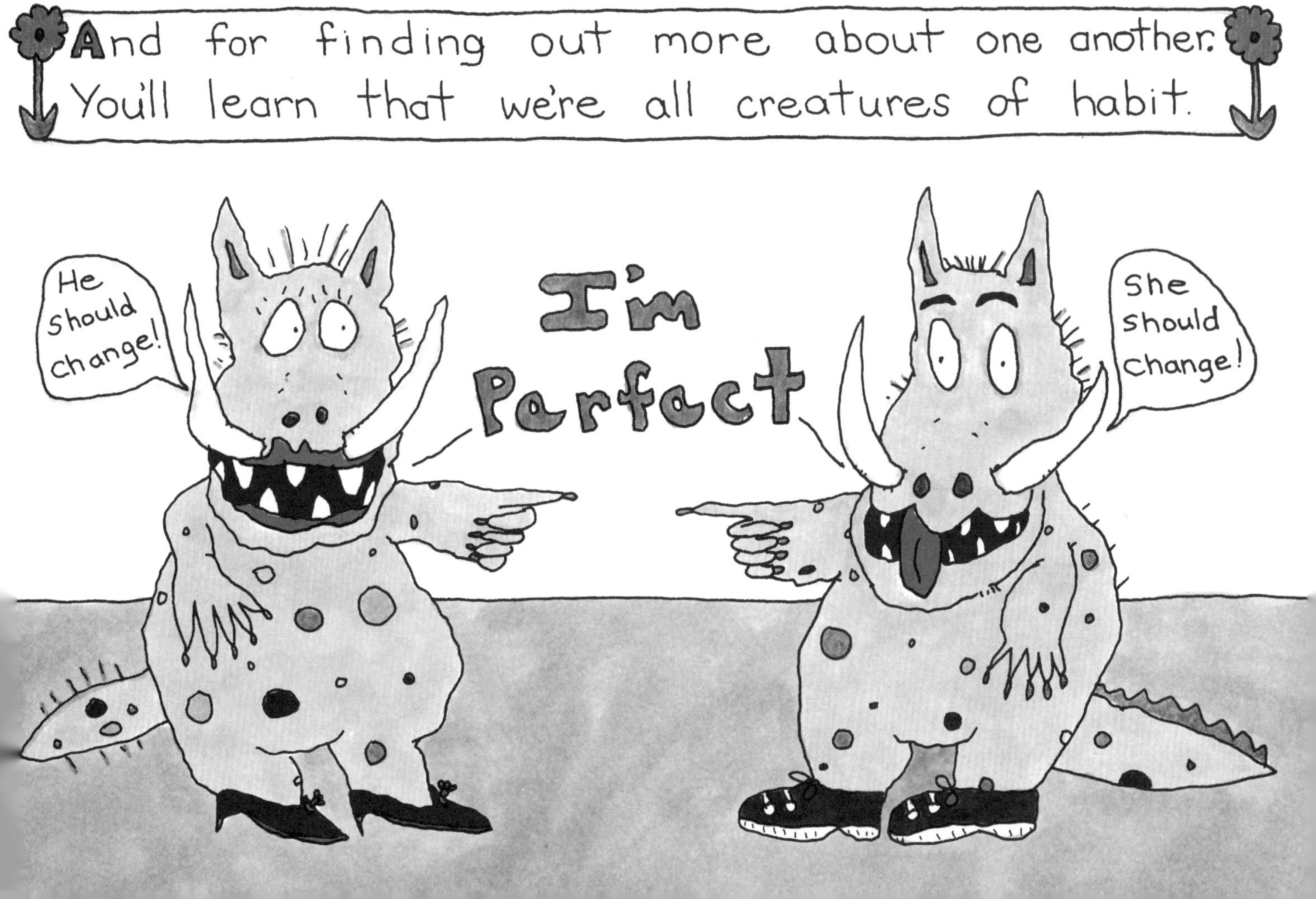
He should change!
I'm Perfect
She should change!

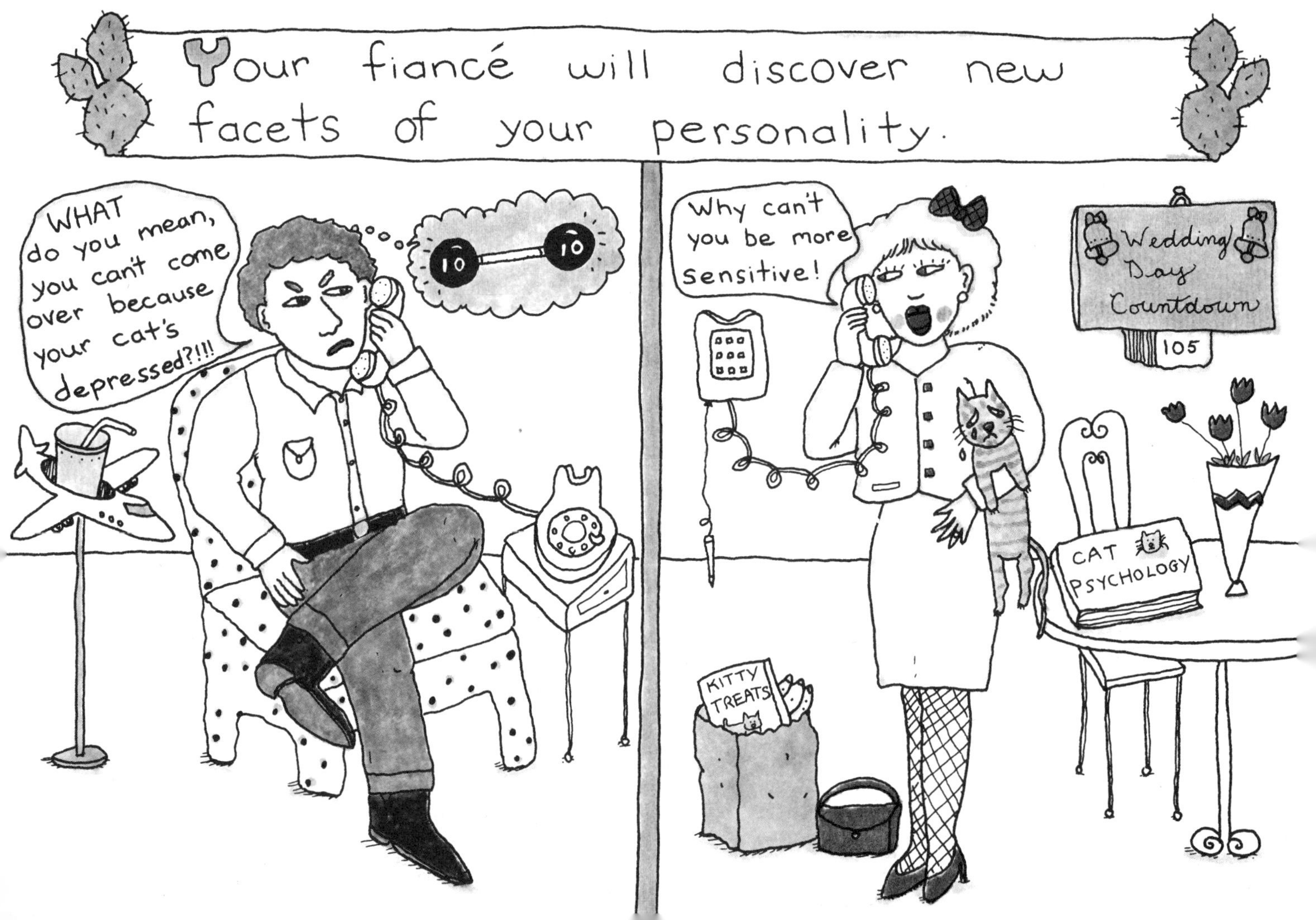
Your fiancé will discover new facets of your personality.
WHAT do you mean, you can't come over because your cat's depressed?!!!
10 10
Why can't you be more sensitive!
Wedding Day Countdown
105
CAT PSYCHOLOGY
KITTY TREATS

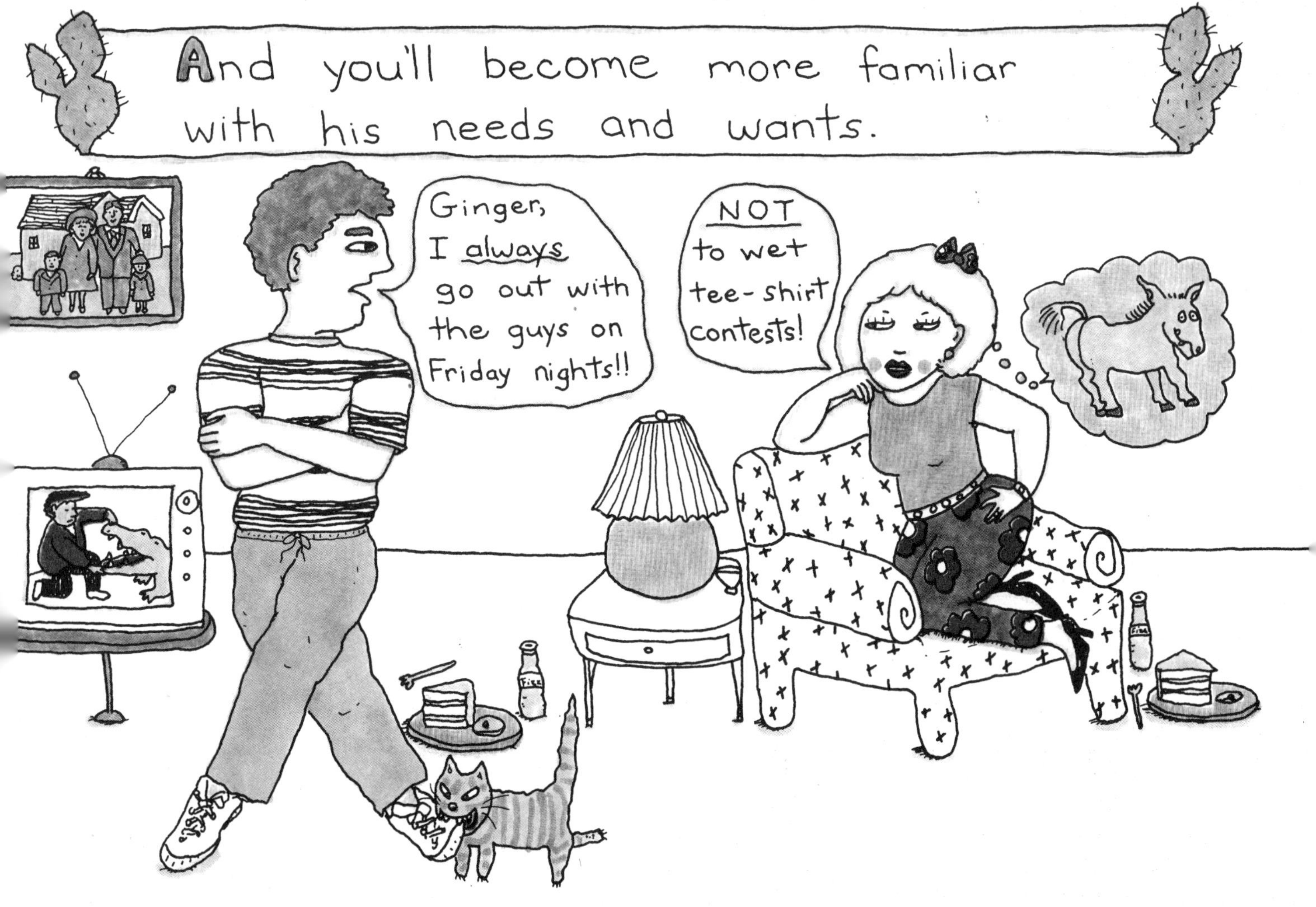
And you'll become more familiar with his needs and wants.
Ginger, I always go out with the guys on Friday nights!!
NOT to wet tee-shirt contests!

You may not agree on everything, but together you will learn the fine art of compromise.

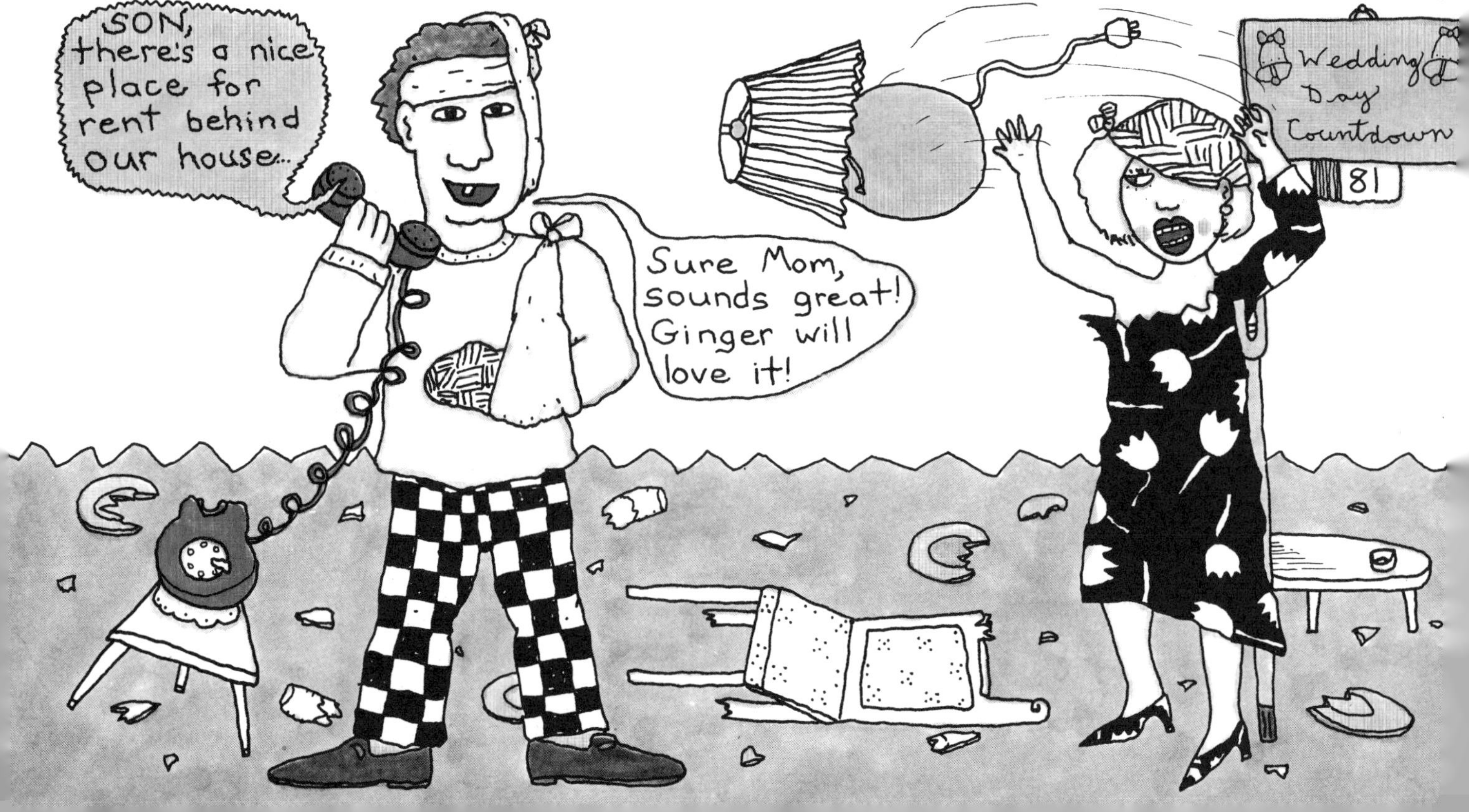
SON, there's a nice place for rent behind our house...
Sure Mom, sounds great! Ginger will love it!
Wedding Day Countdown
81

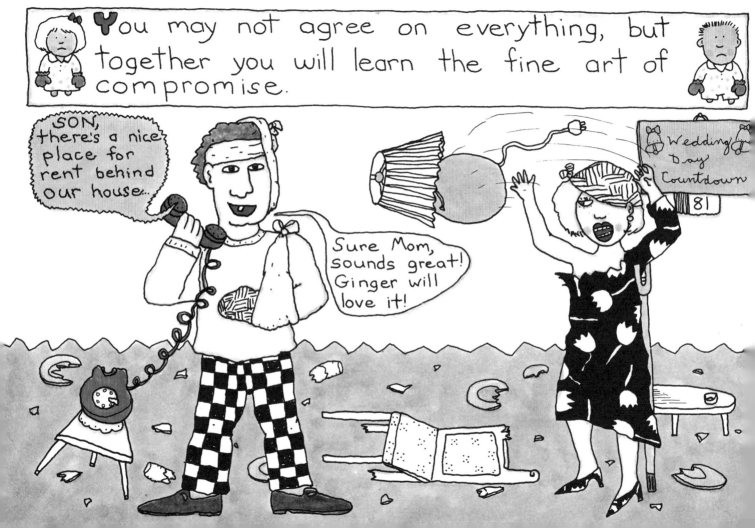

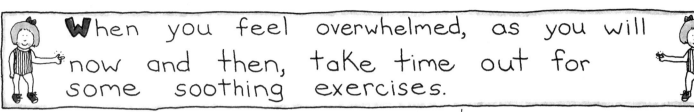

When you feel overwhelmed, as you will now and then, take time out for some soothing exercises.

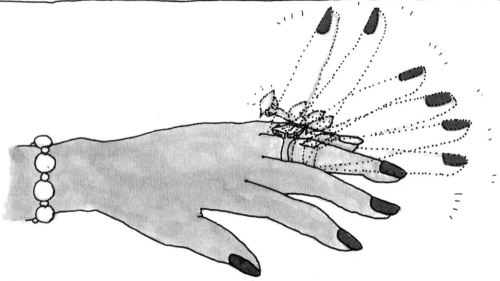

Lift your ring finger up and down, up and down, up and down, up and down, up and down....

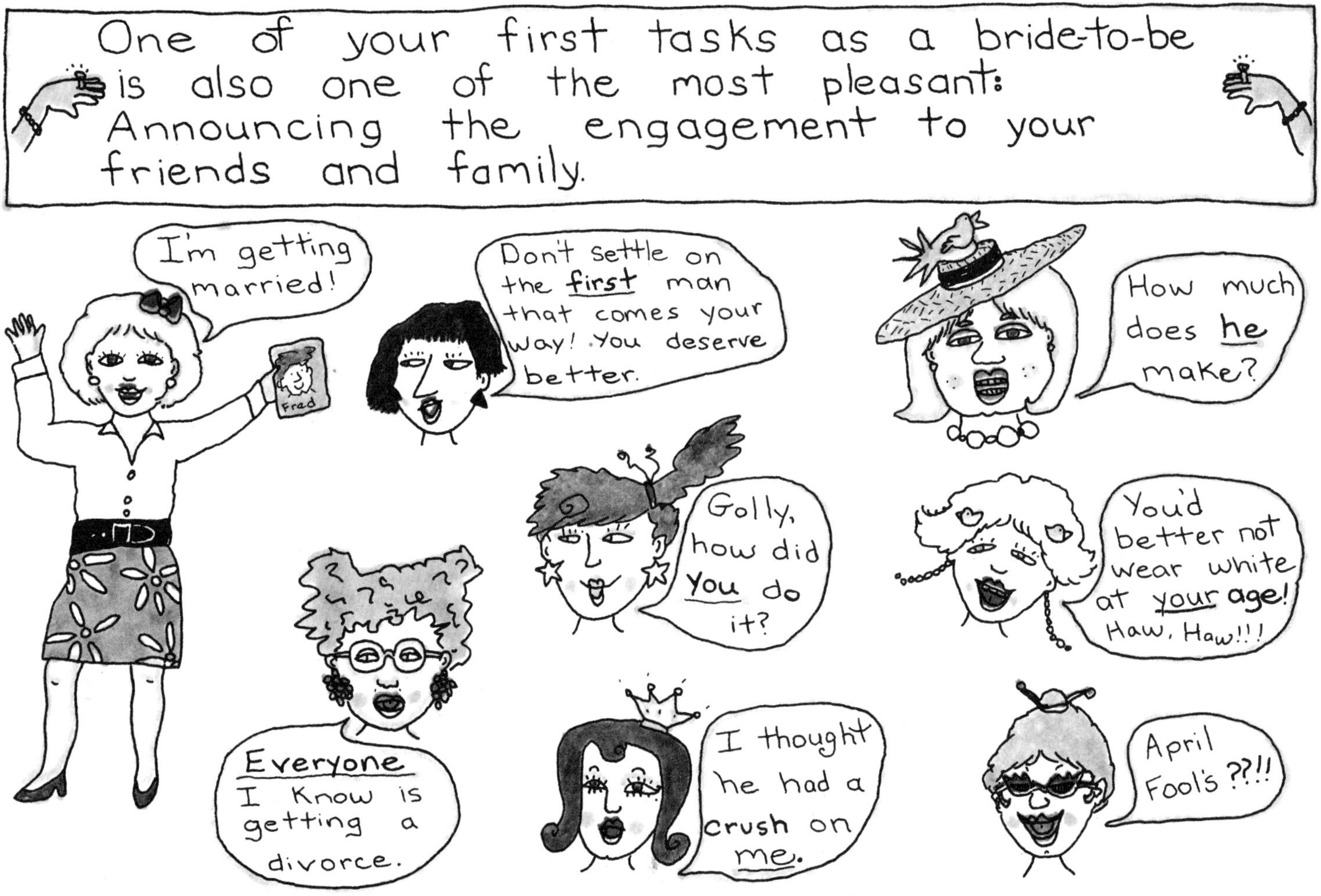
One of your first tasks as a bride-to-be is also one of the most pleasant: Announcing the engagement to your friends and family.
I'm getting married!
Fred
Don't settle on the first man that comes your way! You deserve better.
How much does he make?
Golly, how did You do it?
You'd better not wear white at your age! Haw, Haw!!!
Everyone I Know is getting a divorce.
I thought he had a crush on me.
April Fool's ??!!

They'll all want to be helpful.

Every decision you make without consulting me puts an axe in my chest!

Ginger, listen to your mother. You'll make her happy and maybe I'll get some sleep!

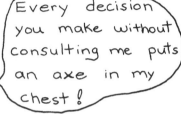

I'm your best friend! Why can't I come on your honeymoon?

As your sister-in-law-to-be, I'd like to loan you my wedding dress!

Can a helpful brother pack your stuff out of my new room?

Did my son tell you, I'm going to sing Fiddler On The Roof during the wedding march?

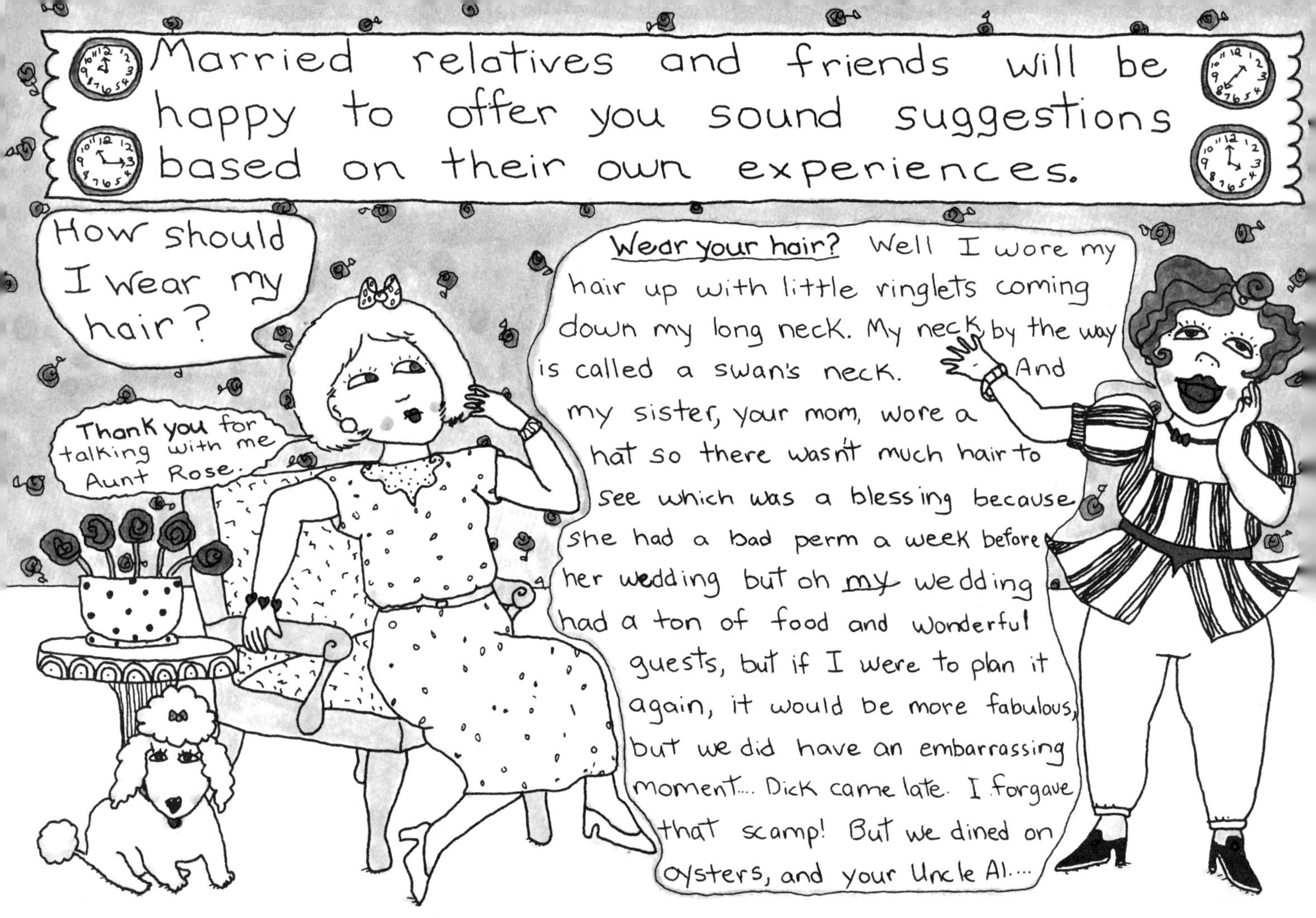
Married relatives and friends will be happy to offer you sound suggestions based on their own experiences.
How should I wear my hair?
Thank you for talking with me Aunt Rose.
Wear your hair? Well I wore my hair up with little ringlets coming down my long neck. My neck, by the way is called a swan's neck. And my sister, your mom, wore a hat so there wasn't much hair to see which was a blessing because she had a bad perm a week before her wedding but oh my wedding had a ton of food and wonderful guests, but if I were to plan it again, it would be more fabulous, but we did have an embarrassing moment.... Dick came late. I forgave that scamp! But we dined on oysters, and your Uncle Al....

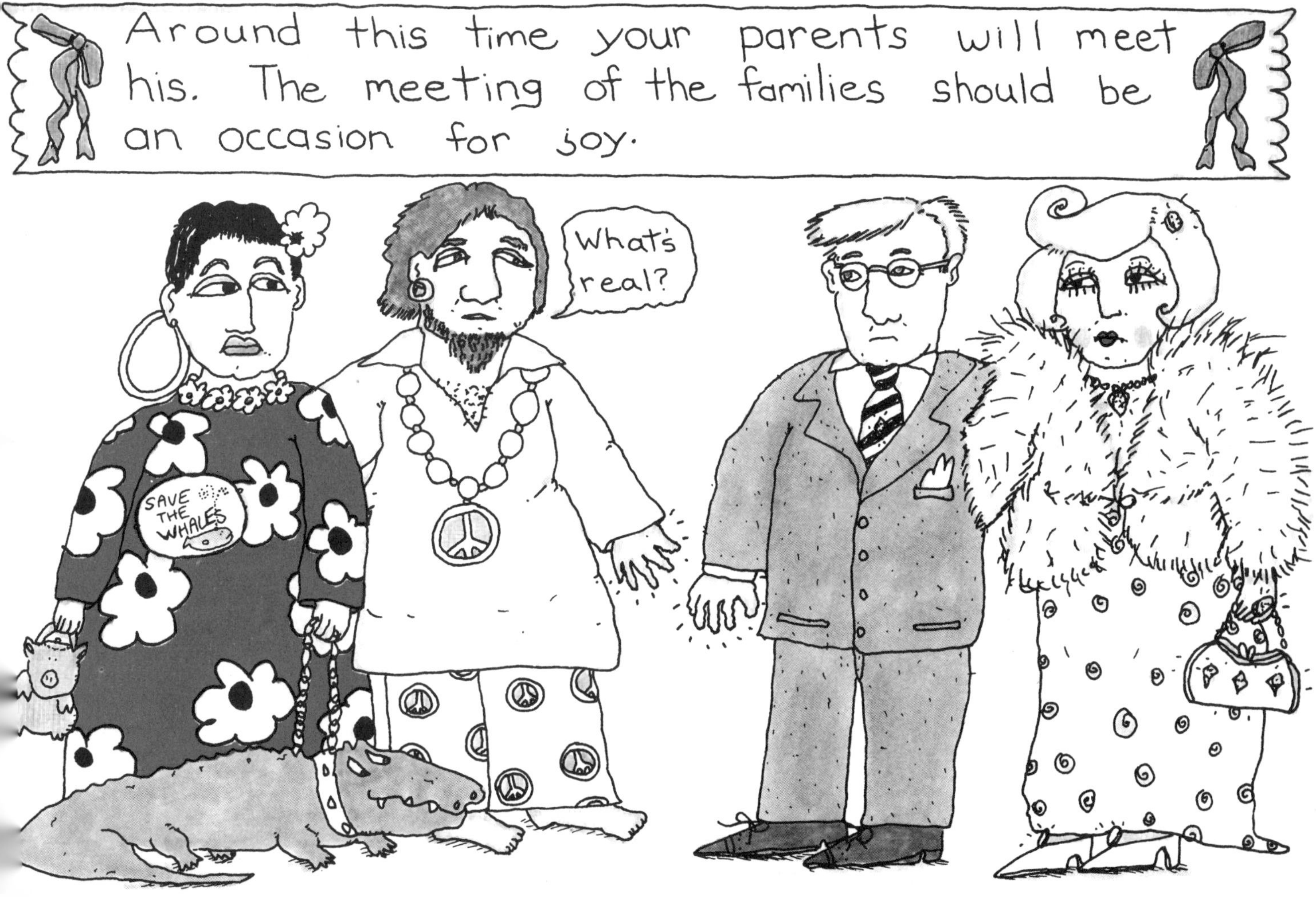
Around this time your parents will meet his. The meeting of the families should be an occasion for joy.
What's real?
SAVE THE WHALES

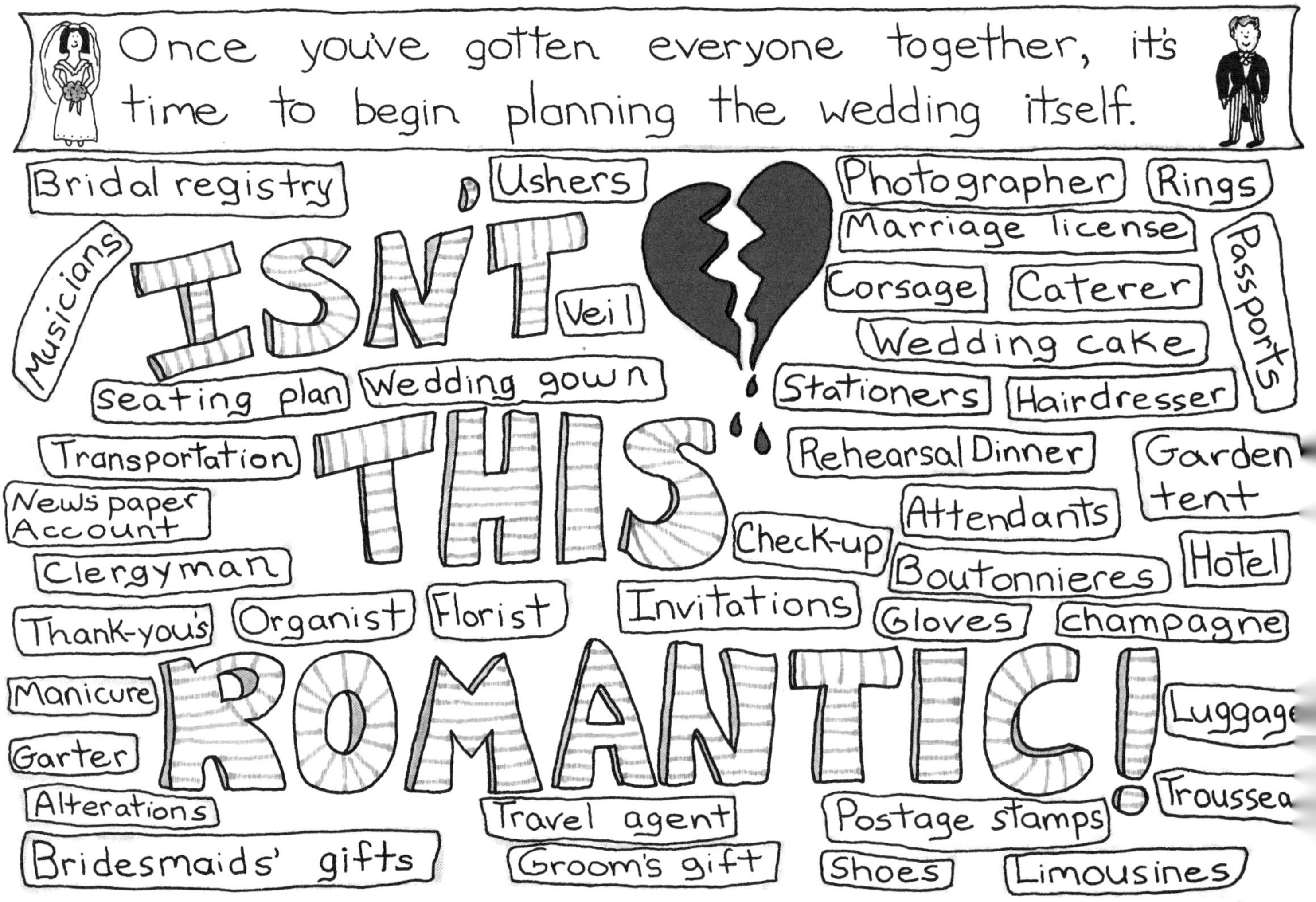
Once you've gotten everyone together, it's time to begin planning the wedding itself.
ISN'T THIS ROMANTIC!
Bridal registry
Ushers
Photographer
Rings
Marriage license
Passports
Musicians
Veil
Corsage
Caterer
Wedding cake
seating plan
Wedding gown
Stationers
Hairdresser
Transportation
Rehearsal Dinner
Garden tent
Newspaper Account
Attendants
Check-up
Clergyman
Boutonnieres
Hotel
Thank-you's
Organist
Florist
Invitations
Gloves
champagne
Manicure
Luggag
Garter
Troussea
Alterations
Travel agent
Postage stamps
Bridesmaids' gifts
Groom's gift
Shoes
Limousines

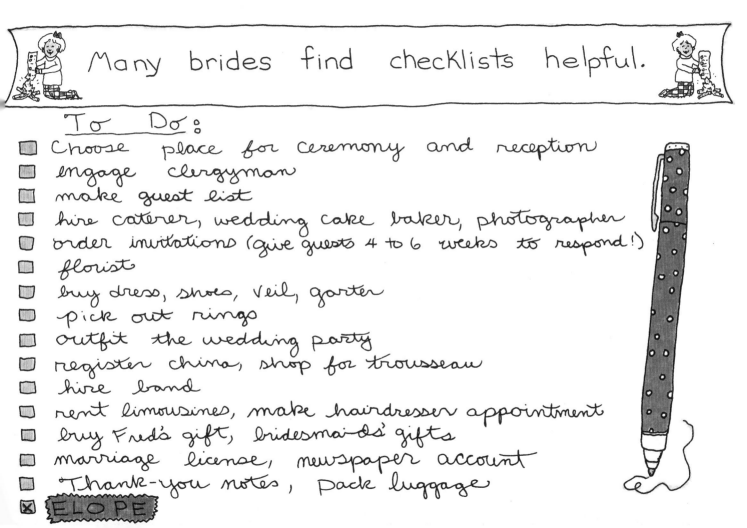

Many brides find checklists helpful.

To Do:

- ☐ Choose place for ceremony and reception
- ☐ engage clergyman
- ☐ make guest list
- ☐ hire caterer, wedding cake baker, photographer
- ☐ order invitations (give guests 4 to 6 weeks to respond!)
- ☐ florist
- ☐ buy dress, shoes, veil, garter
- ☐ pick out rings
- ☐ outfit the wedding party
- ☐ register china, shop for trousseau
- ☐ hire band
- ☐ rent limousines, make hairdresser appointment
- ☐ buy Fred's gift, bridesmaids' gifts
- ☐ marriage license, newspaper account
- ☐ Thank-you notes, pack luggage
- ☒ ELOPE

Coordinate your guest lists carefully.

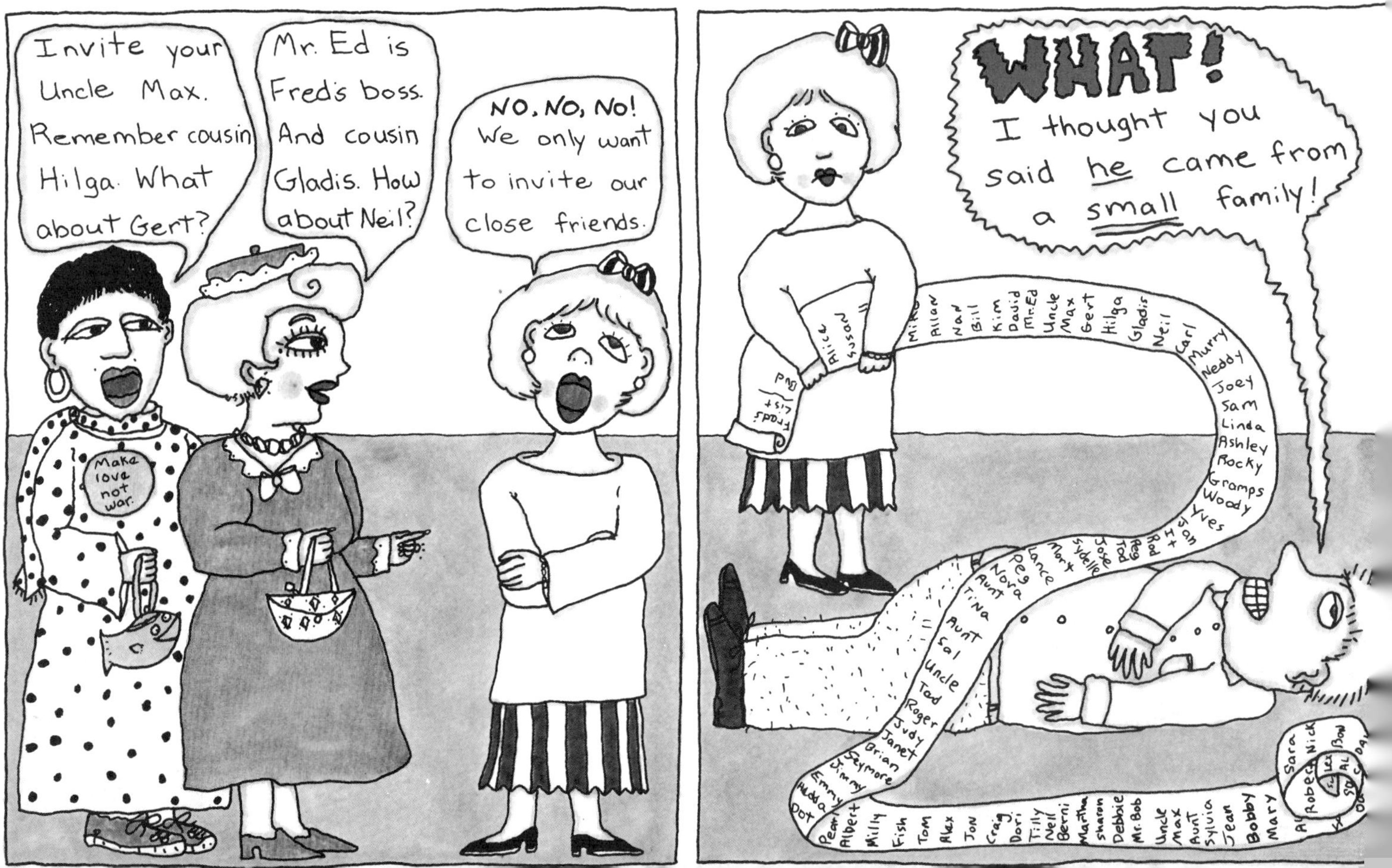
Invite your Uncle Max. Remember cousin Hilga. What about Gert?
Mr. Ed is Fred's boss. And cousin Gladis. How about Neil?
NO, NO, No! We only want to invite our close friends.
Make love not war.
WHAT! I thought you said he came from a small family!
Fred's List

Make certain the invitations are exactly right.

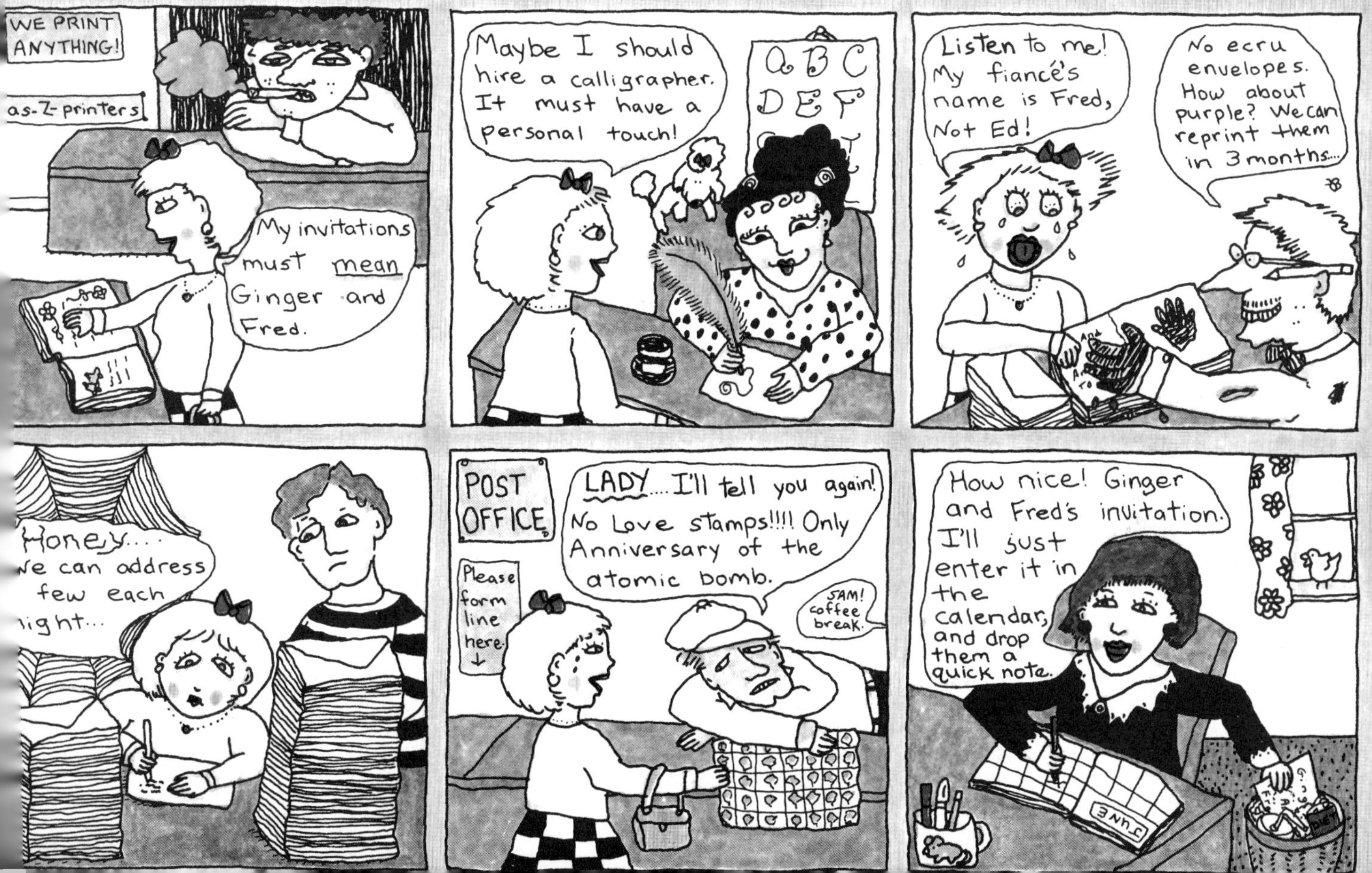

WE PRINT ANYTHING!
as-Z-printers
My invitations must mean Ginger and Fred.
Maybe I should hire a calligrapher. It must have a personal touch!
Listen to me! My fiancé's name is Fred, Not Ed!
No ecru envelopes. How about purple? We can reprint them in 3 months....
Honey... we can address few each night...
POST OFFICE
Please form line here. ↓
LADY.... I'll tell you again! No Love stamps!!!! Only Anniversary of the atomic bomb.
SAM! coffee break.
How nice! Ginger and Fred's invitation. I'll just enter it in the calendar, and drop them a quick note.

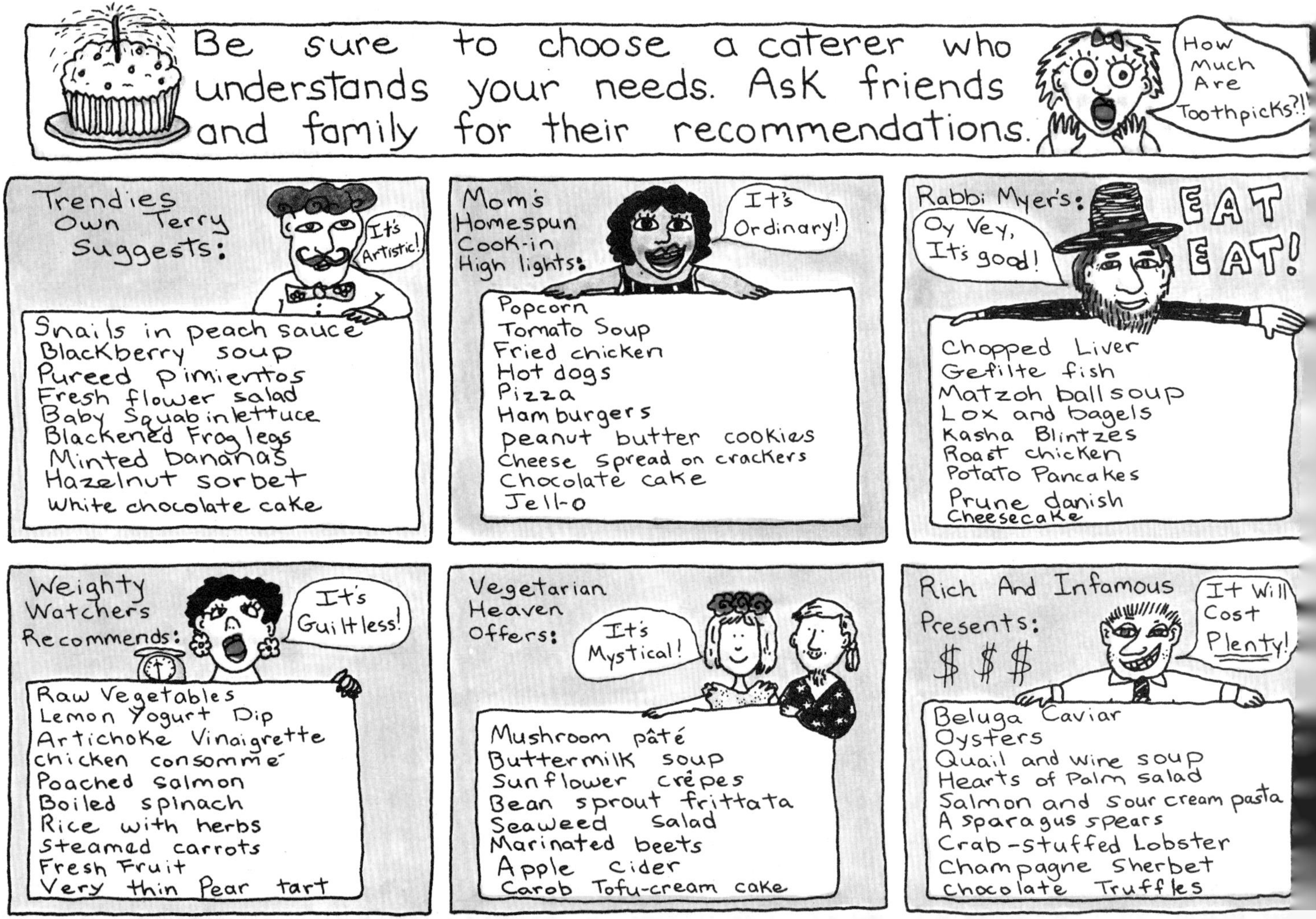
Be sure to choose a caterer who understands your needs. Ask friends and family for their recommendations.
How Much Are Toothpicks?!!
Trendies Own Terry Suggests:
It's Artistic!
Snails in peach sauce
Blackberry soup
Pureed pimientos
Fresh flower salad
Baby Squab in lettuce
Blackened Frog legs
Minted bananas
Hazelnut sorbet
White chocolate cake
Mom's Homespun Cook-in Highlights:
It's Ordinary!
Popcorn
Tomato Soup
Fried chicken
Hot dogs
Pizza
Hamburgers
peanut butter cookies
Cheese spread on crackers
Chocolate cake
Jell-o
Rabbi Myer's:
Oy Vey, It's good!
EAT EAT!
Chopped Liver
Gefilte fish
Matzoh ball soup
Lox and bagels
Kasha Blintzes
Roast chicken
Potato Pancakes
Prune danish
Cheesecake
Weighty Watchers Recommends:
It's Guiltless!
Raw Vegetables
Lemon Yogurt Dip
Artichoke Vinaigrette
chicken consommé
Poached salmon
Boiled spinach
Rice with herbs
Steamed carrots
Fresh Fruit
Very thin Pear tart
Vegetarian Heaven Offers:
It's Mystical!
Mushroom pâté
Buttermilk soup
Sunflower crêpes
Bean sprout frittata
Seaweed Salad
Marinated beets
Apple cider
Carob Tofu-cream cake
Rich And Infamous Presents:
$ $ $
It Will Cost Plenty!
Beluga Caviar
Oysters
Quail and wine soup
Hearts of Palm salad
Salmon and sour cream pasta
Asparagus spears
Crab-stuffed Lobster
Champagne Sherbet
chocolate Truffles

Before you begin searching for that perfect dress, you'll need to decide what Kind of bride you are. Visualize yourself in different settings.

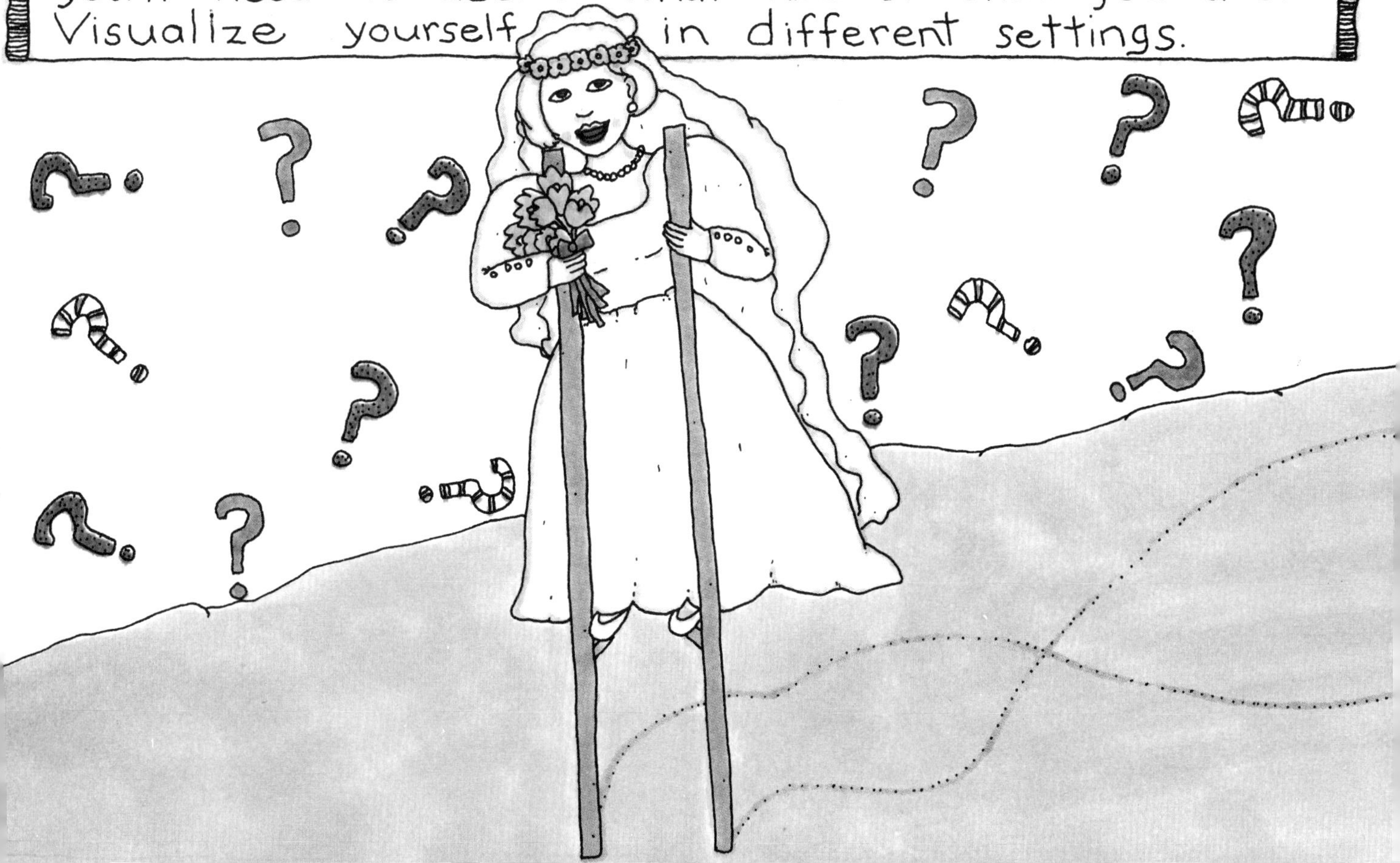

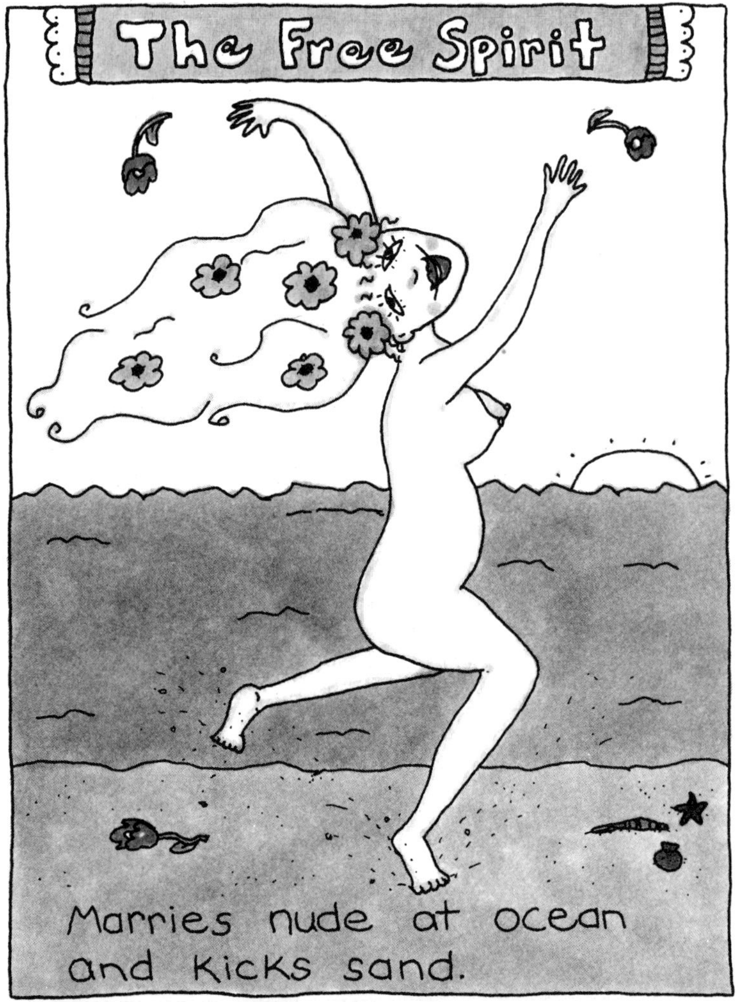
The Free Spirit

Marries nude at ocean and kicks sand.

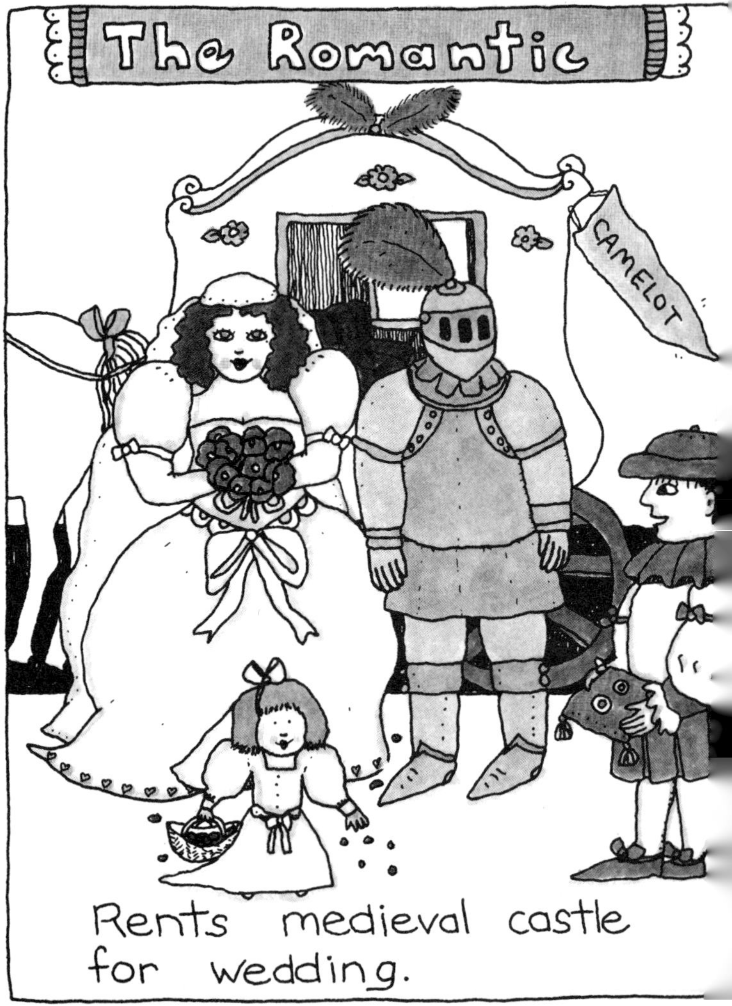
The Romantic
CAMELOT

Rents medieval castle for wedding.

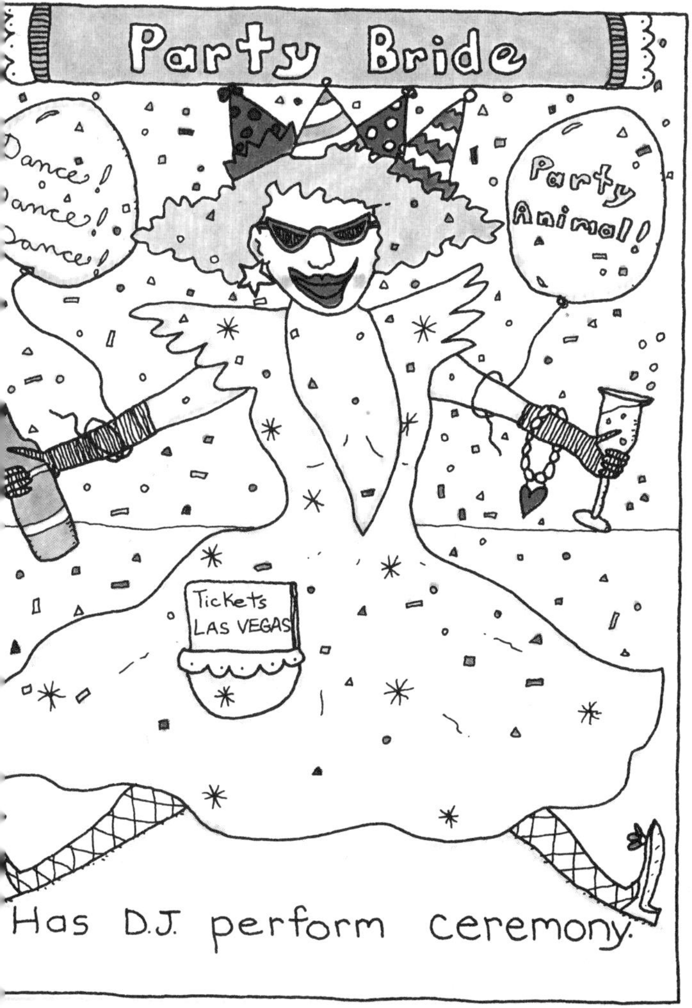
Party Bride
Dance! Dance! Dance!
Party Animal!
Tickets LAS VEGAS
Has D.J. perform ceremony.

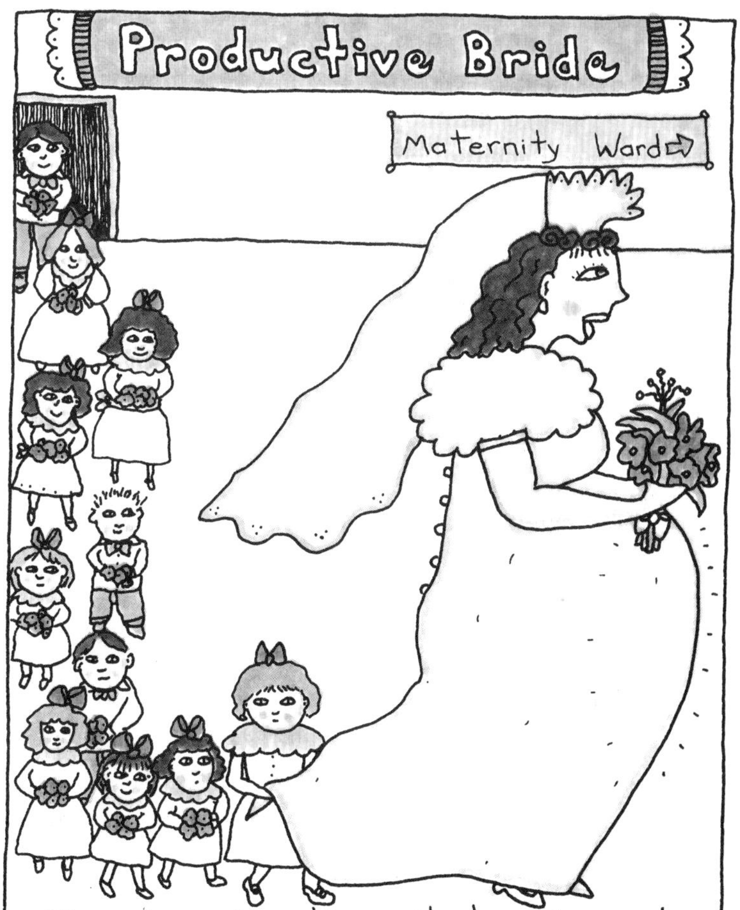
Productive Bride
Maternity Ward
Marries in hospital chapel.

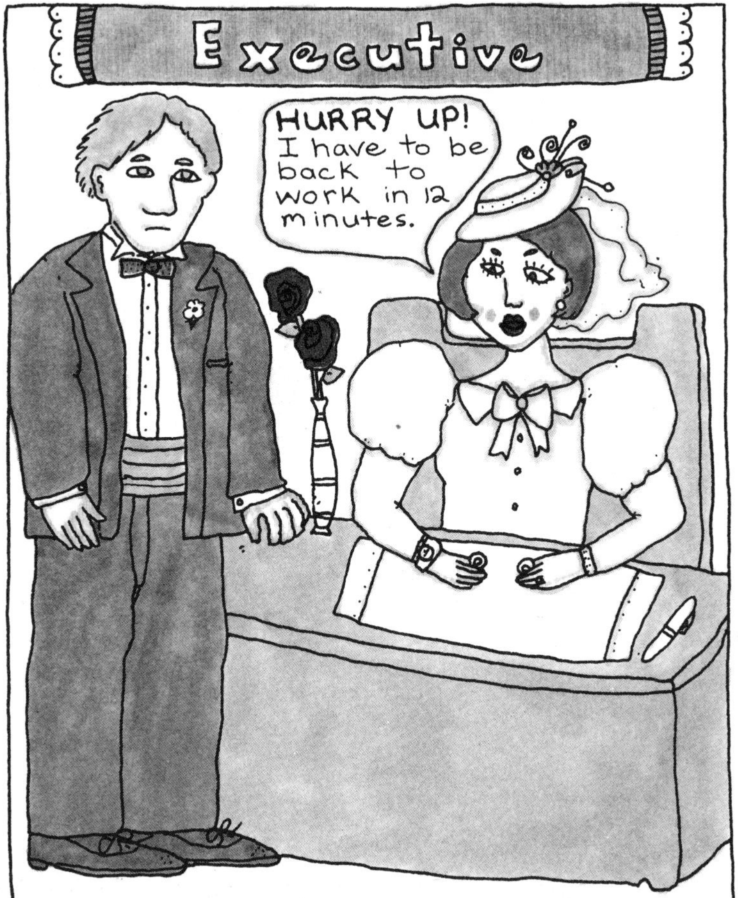
Executive
HURRY UP! I have to be back to work in 12 minutes.

Hires another couple to go on honeymoon.

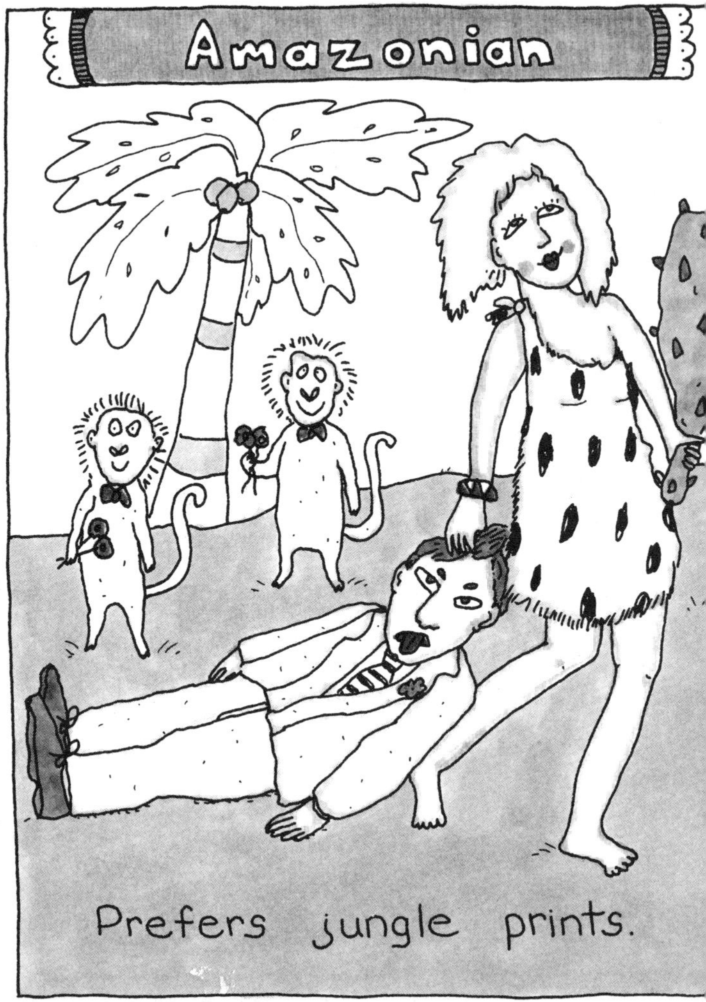
Amazonian

Prefers jungle prints.

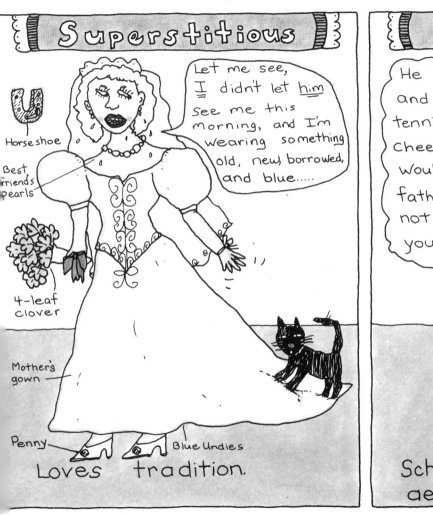

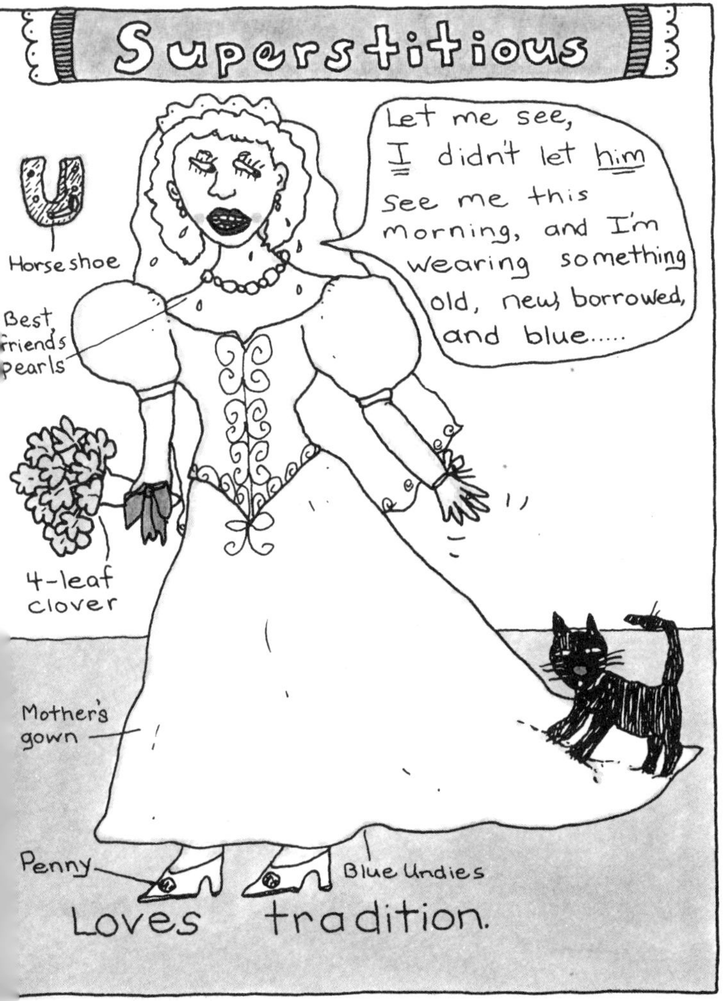
Superstitious
Let me see, I didn't let him see me this morning, and I'm wearing something old, new, borrowed, and blue.....
Horseshoe
Best friend's pearls
4-leaf clover
Mother's gown
Penny
Blue Undies
Loves tradition.

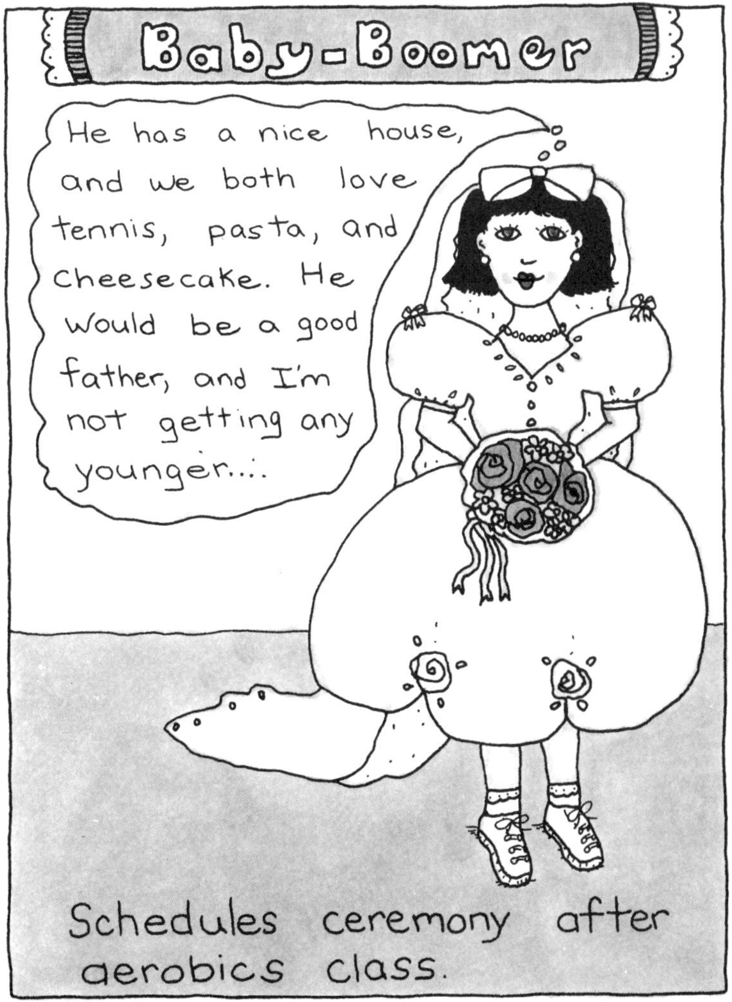
Baby-Boomer
He has a nice house, and we both love tennis, pasta, and cheesecake. He would be a good father, and I'm not getting any younger....
Schedules ceremony after aerobics class.

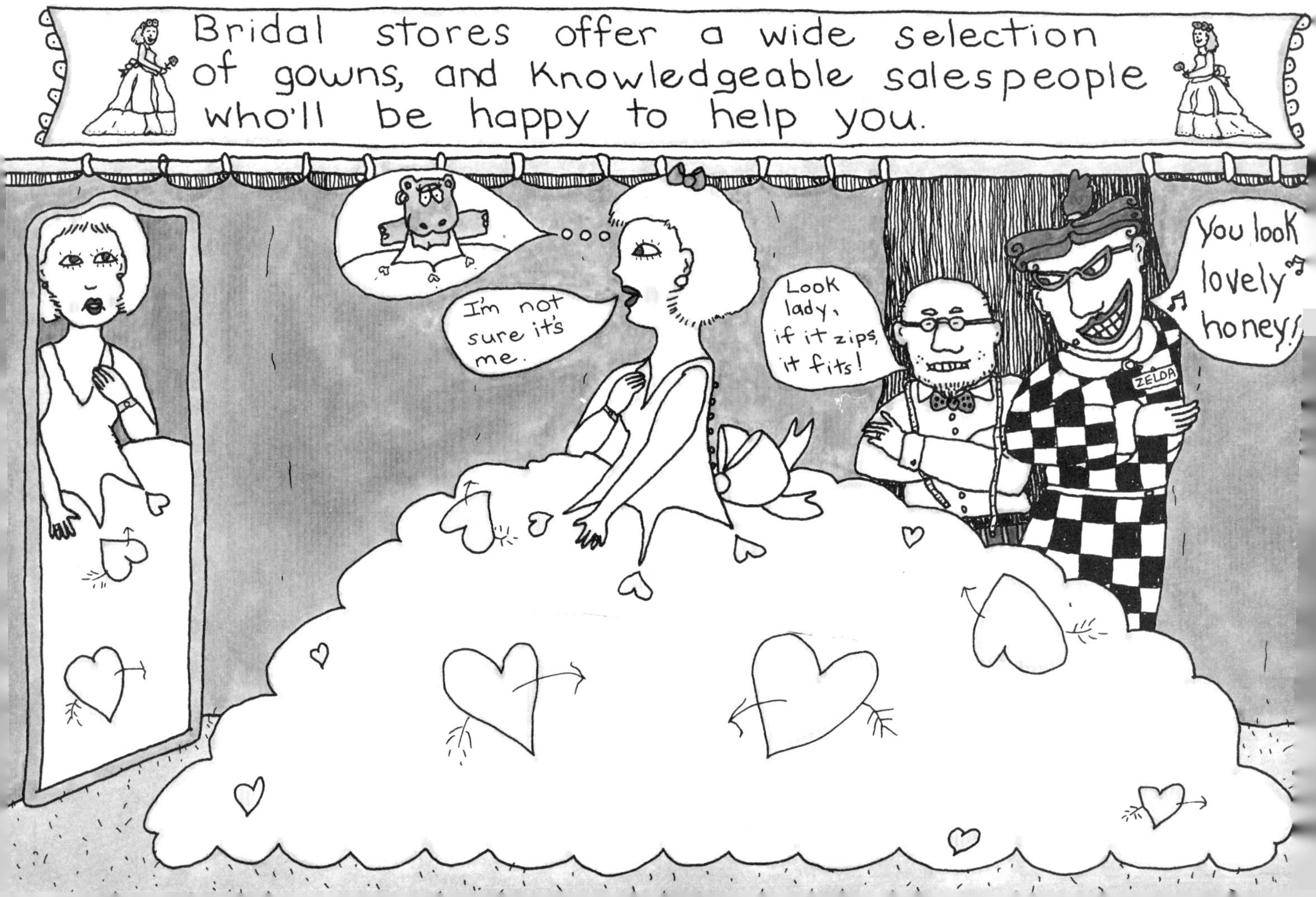
Bridal stores offer a wide selection of gowns, and Knowledgeable salespeople who'll be happy to help you.
I'm not sure it's me.
Look lady, if it zips, it fits!
ZELDA
You look lovely honey!

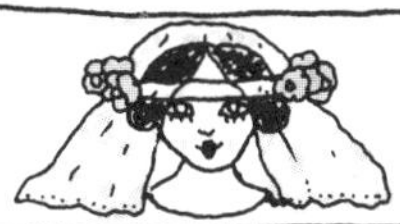

Choose a headpiece that's both appropriate and flattering.

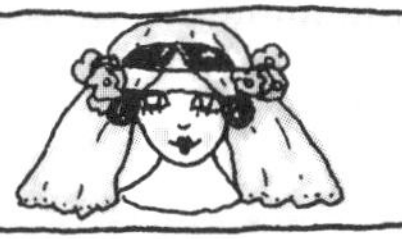

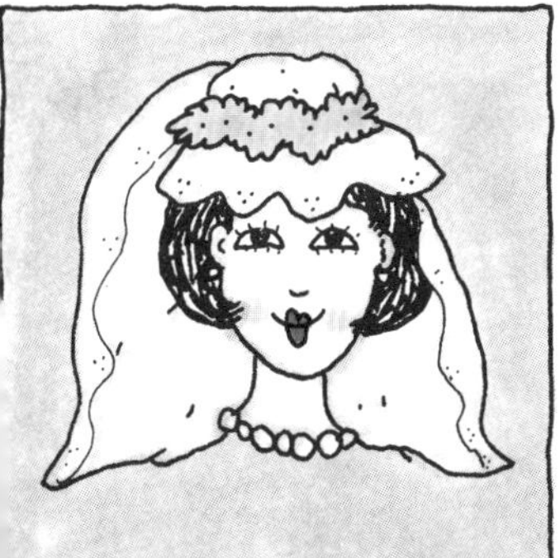

Traditional Charmer

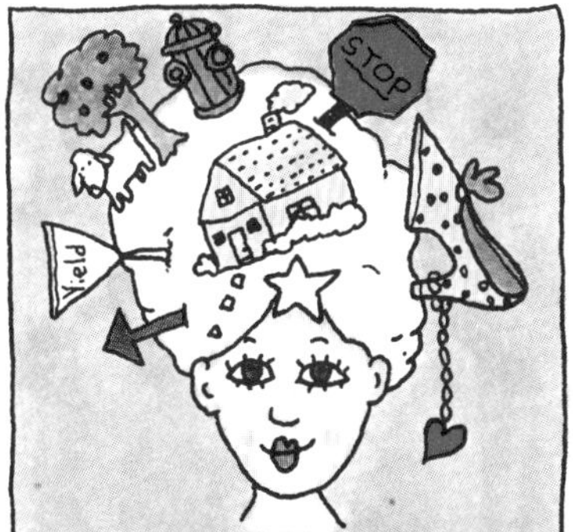
STOP
Yield

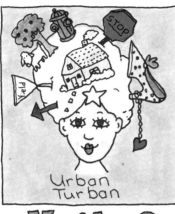

Urban Turban

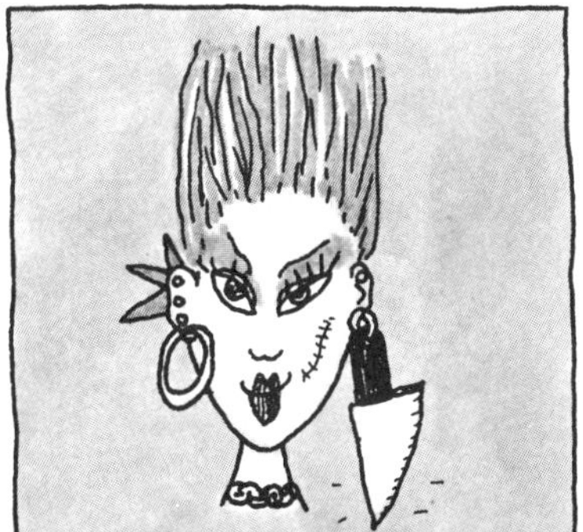

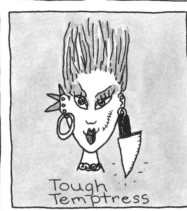

Tough Temptress

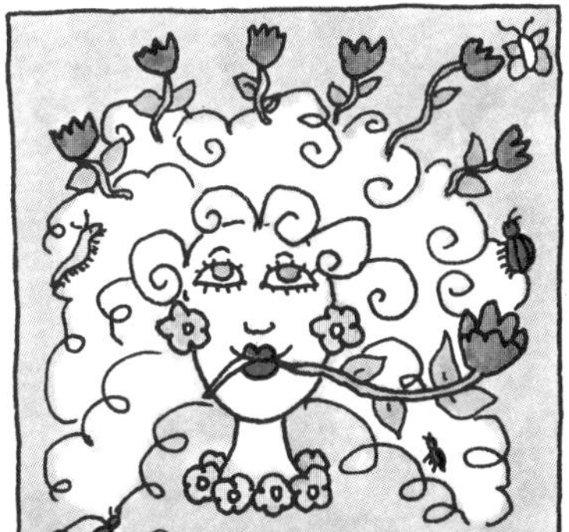

Country Enchantment

To Veil Or Not to Veil

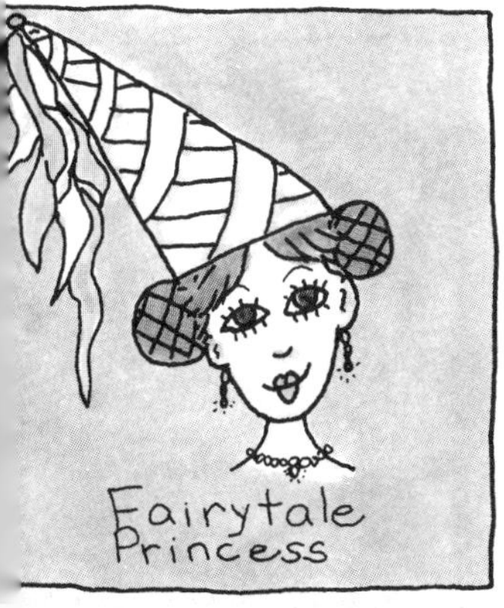

Fairytale Princess

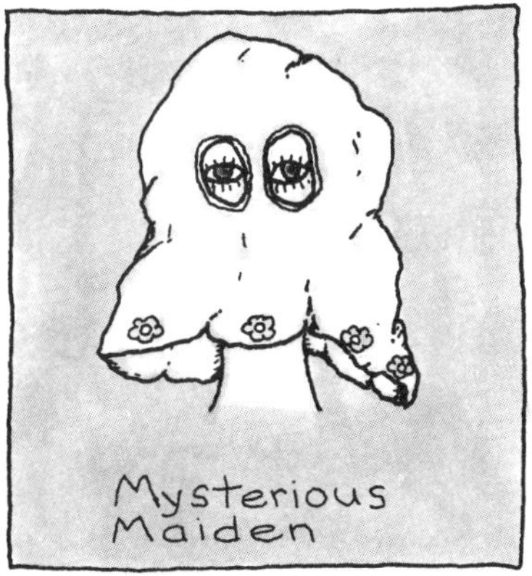

Mysterious Maiden

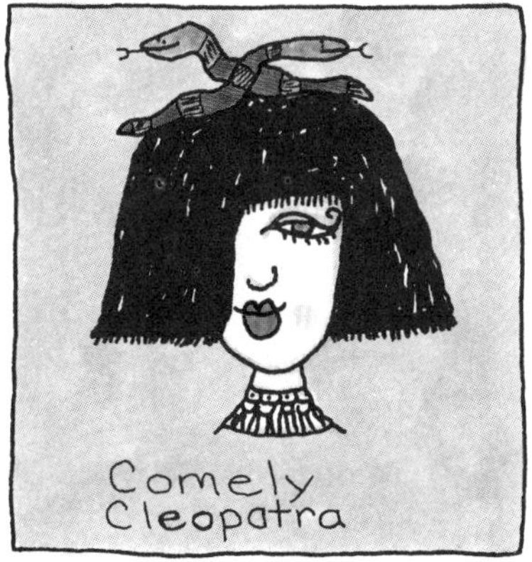

Comely Cleopatra

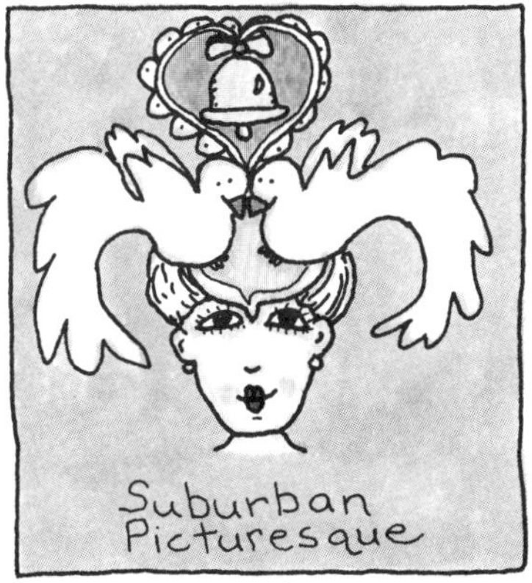

Suburban Picturesque

 And make sure the flowers complement your ensemble.

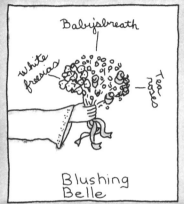

Babyisbreath

White freesias

Tea roses

Blushing Belle

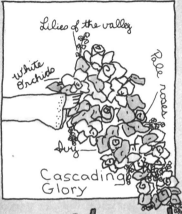

Lilies of the valley

White orchids

Pale roses

Ivy

Cascading Glory

Backyard flowers

Homey Posey

Orange blossom

Jasmine

Gardenia

Heaven Scent

Roses are red and violets are blue...

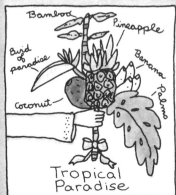

Bamboo

Pineapple

Bird of paradise

Banana Palm

Coconut

Tropical Paradise

Long lasting silk

Eternal beauty

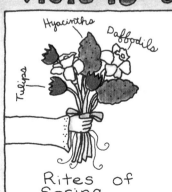

Hyacinths

Daffodils

Tulips

Rites of Spring

Single red rose bought on the way to courthouse

Hasty Hannah

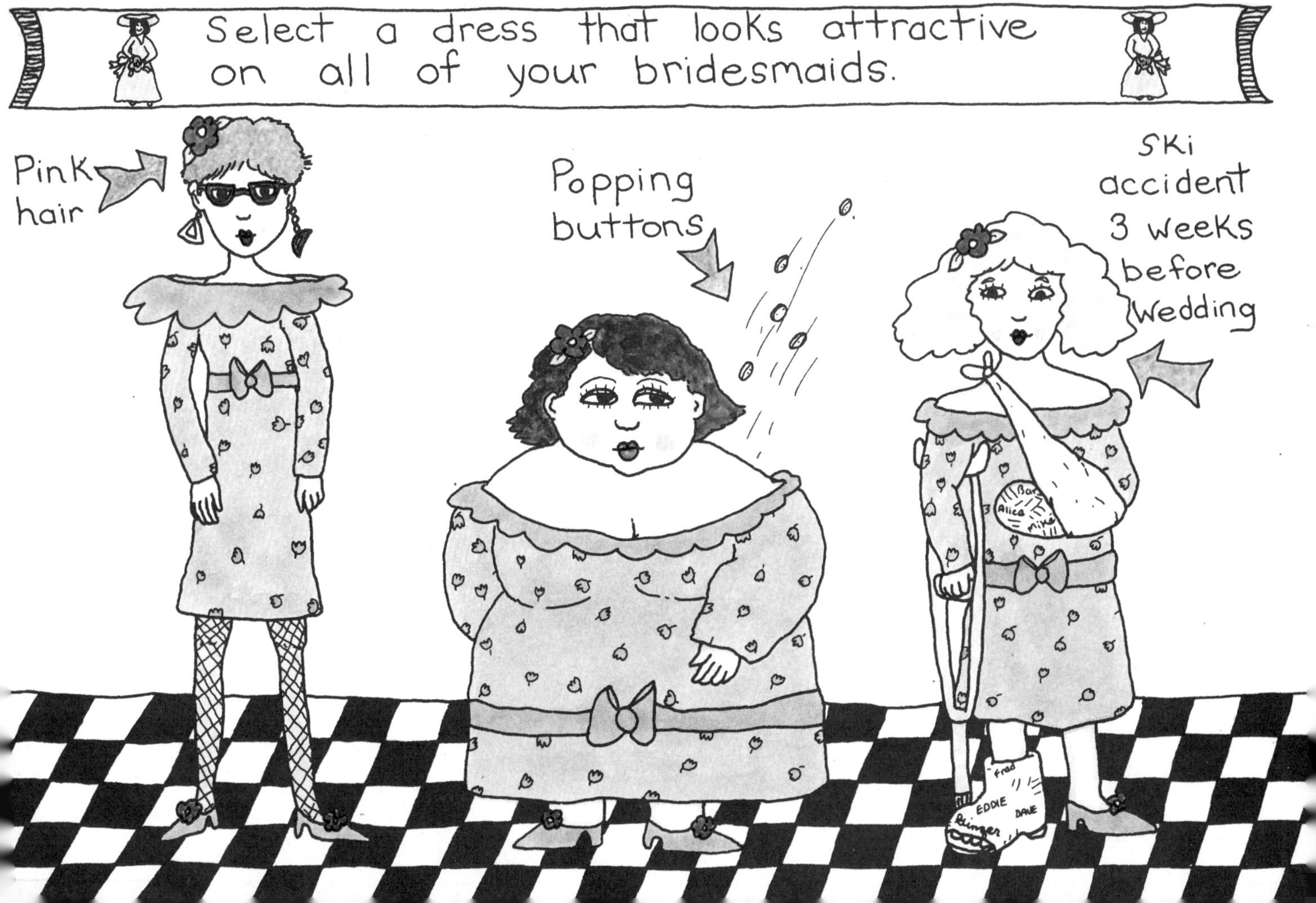

Select a dress that looks attractive on all of your bridesmaids.
Pink hair
Popping buttons
Ski accident 3 weeks before Wedding
Alice
Mike
Fred
EDDIE
DAVE

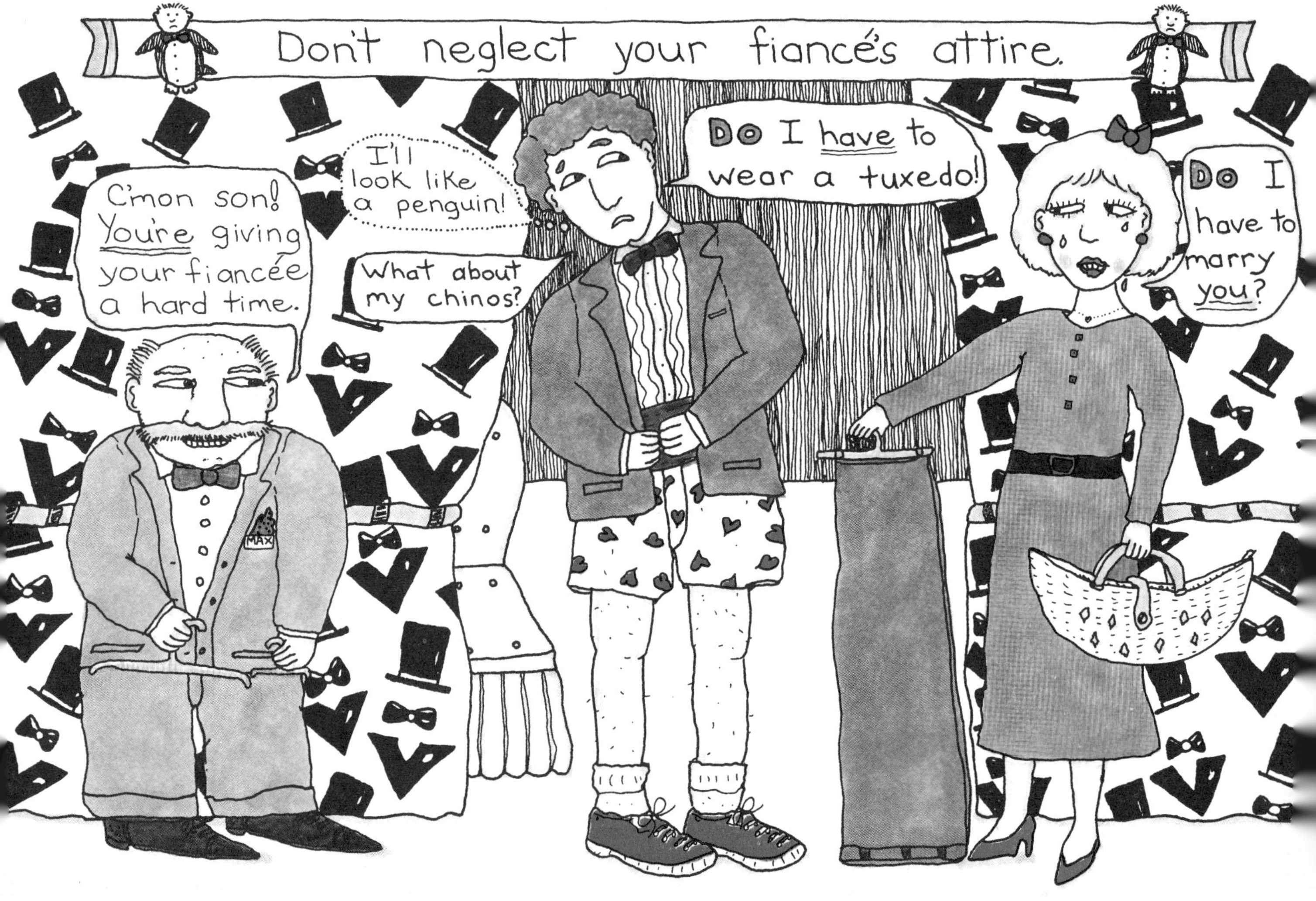
Don't neglect your fiancé's attire.
C'mon son! You're giving your fiancée a hard time.
I'll look like a penguin!
What about my chinos?
Do I have to wear a tuxedo!
Do I have to marry you?
MAX

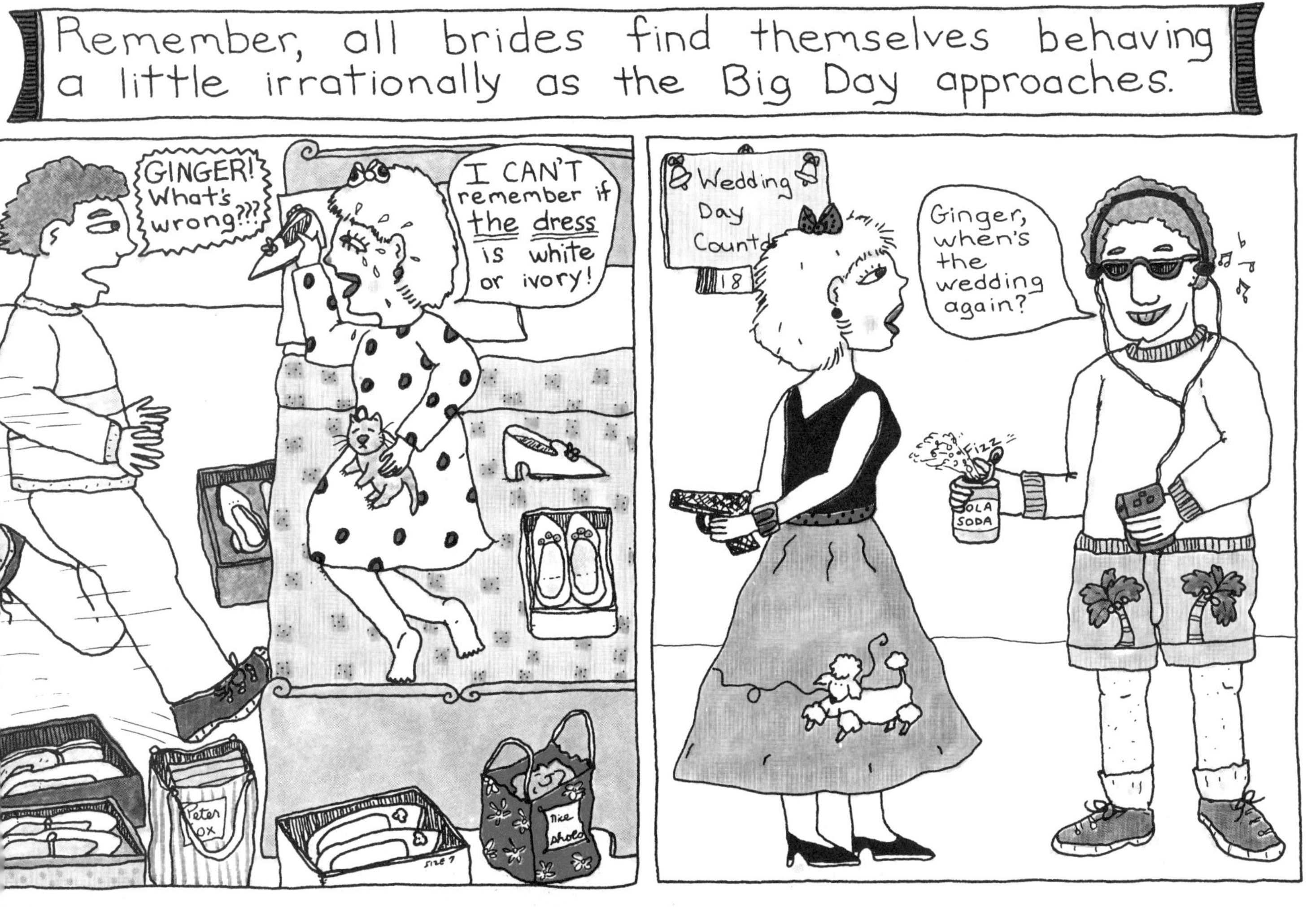
Remember, all brides find themselves behaving a little irrationally as the Big Day approaches.
GINGER! What's wrong???
I CAN'T remember if the dress is white or ivory!
Wedding Day Countd
18
Ginger, when's the wedding again?
FIZZ
OLA SODA

It's perfectly normal to experience tension.

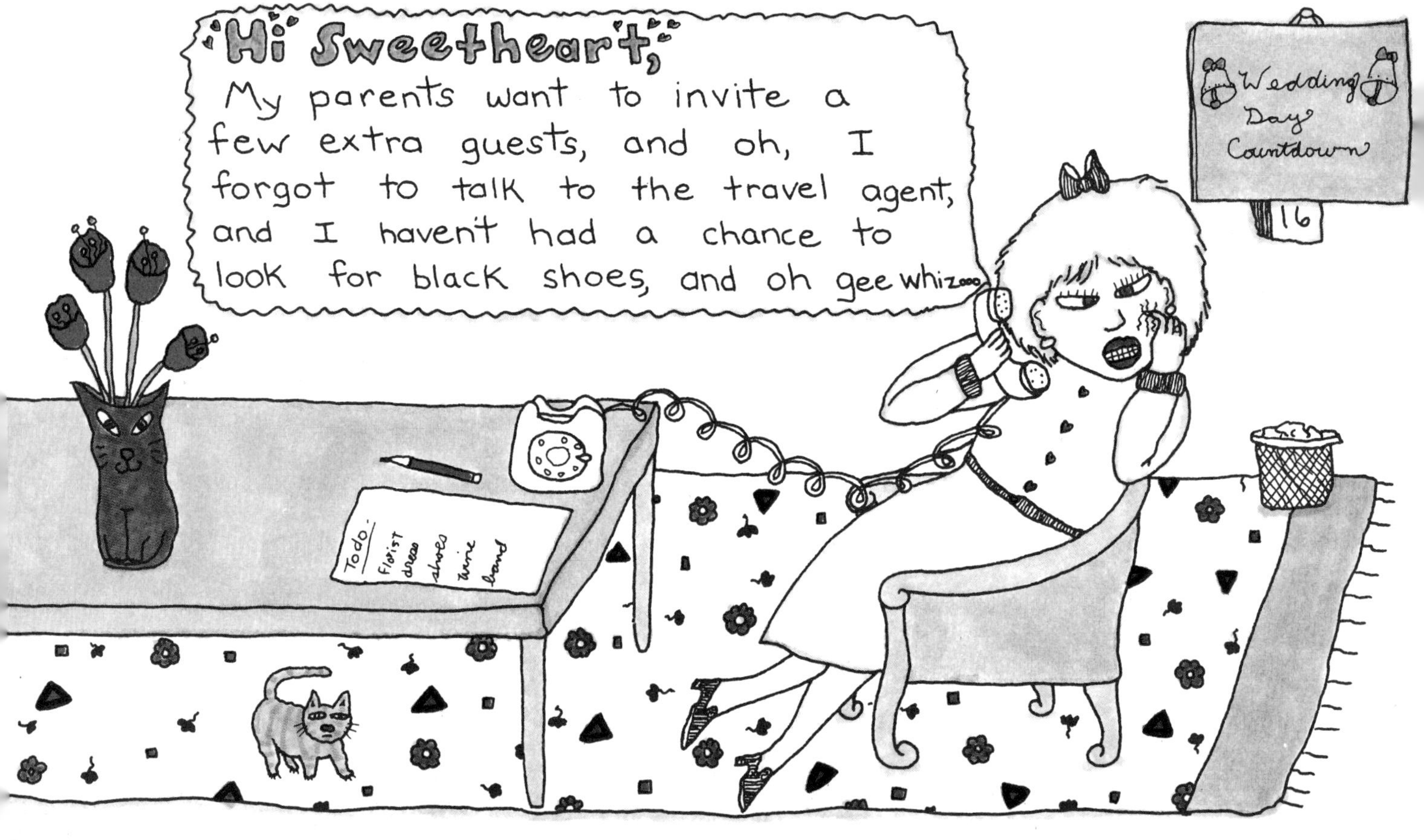
"Hi Sweetheart,
My parents want to invite a few extra guests, and oh, I forgot to talk to the travel agent, and I haven't had a chance to look for black shoes, and oh gee whiz...
Wedding Day Countdown
16
To do:
Florist
dress
shoes
wine
band

Again, you may find exercise helpful.

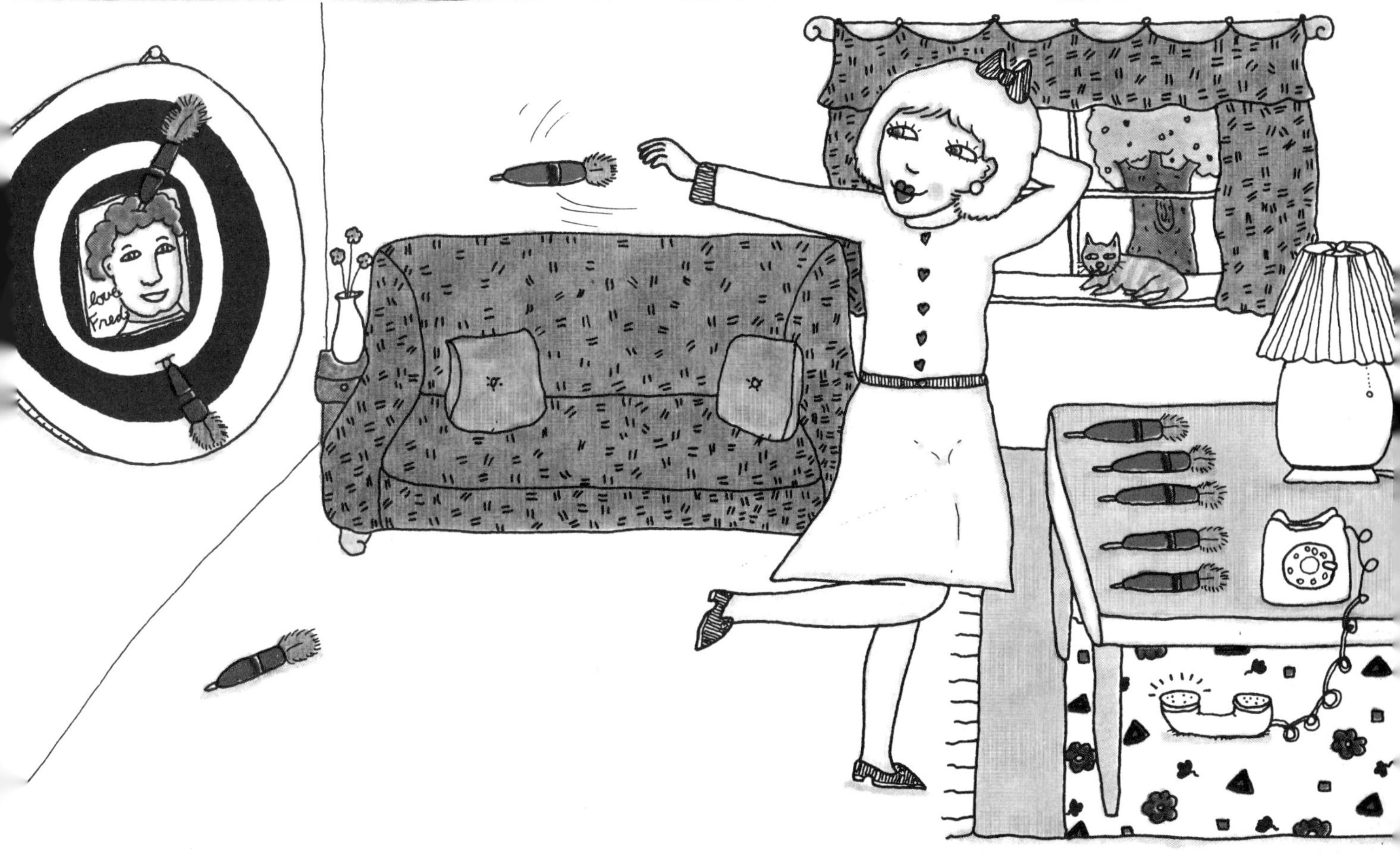
love Fred

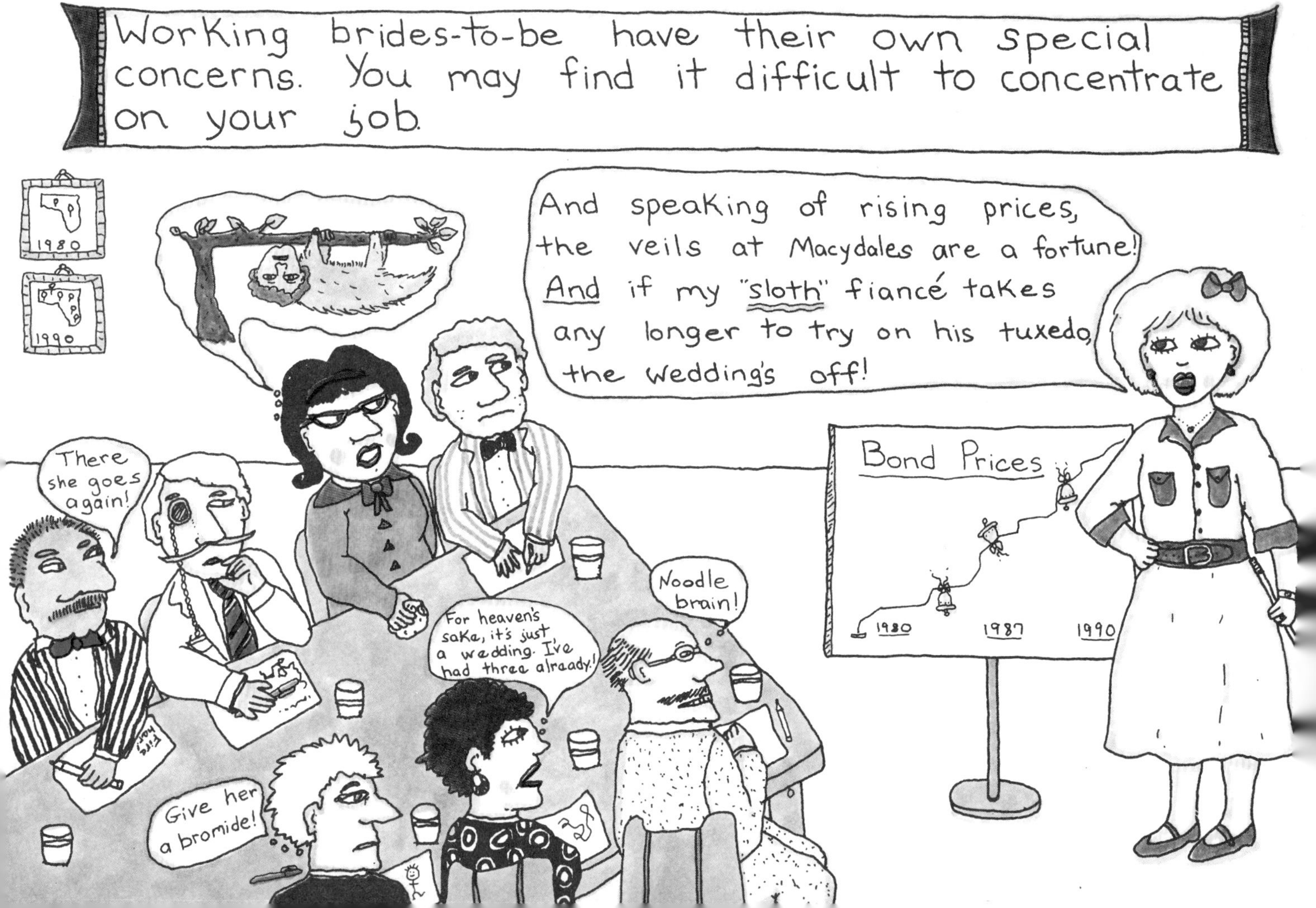
Working brides-to-be have their own special concerns. You may find it difficult to concentrate on your job.
1980
1990
And speaking of rising prices, the veils at Macydales are a fortune! And if my "sloth" fiancé takes any longer to try on his tuxedo, the wedding's off!
Bond Prices
1980
1987
1990
There she goes again!
Noodle brain!
For heaven's sake, it's just a wedding. I've had three already!
Give her a bromide!

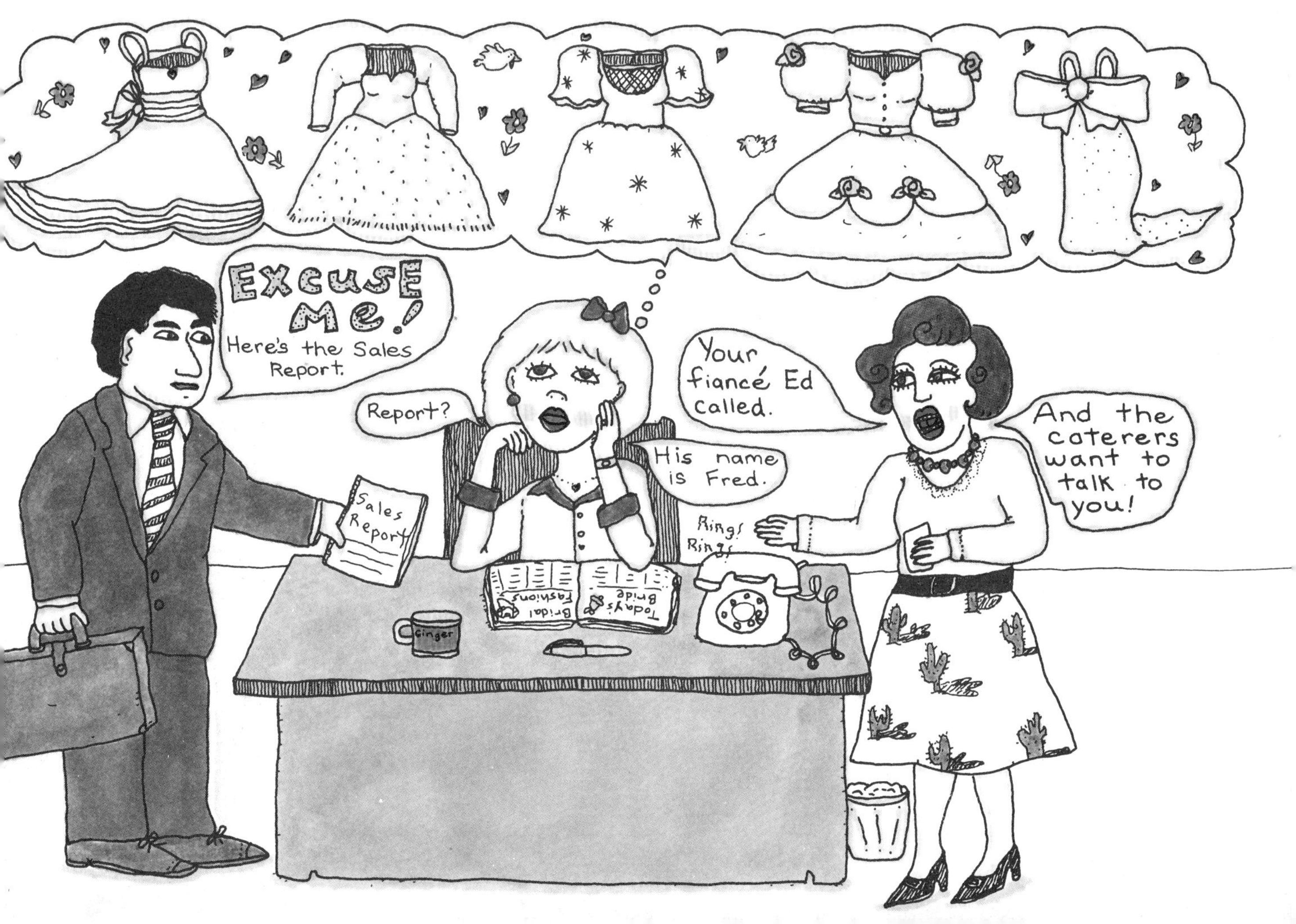
EXCUSE ME!
Here's the Sales Report.
Report?
Your fiancé Ed called.
His name is Fred.
And the caterers want to talk to you!
Rings! Rings!
Sales Report
Today's Bride
Bridal Fashions
Ginger

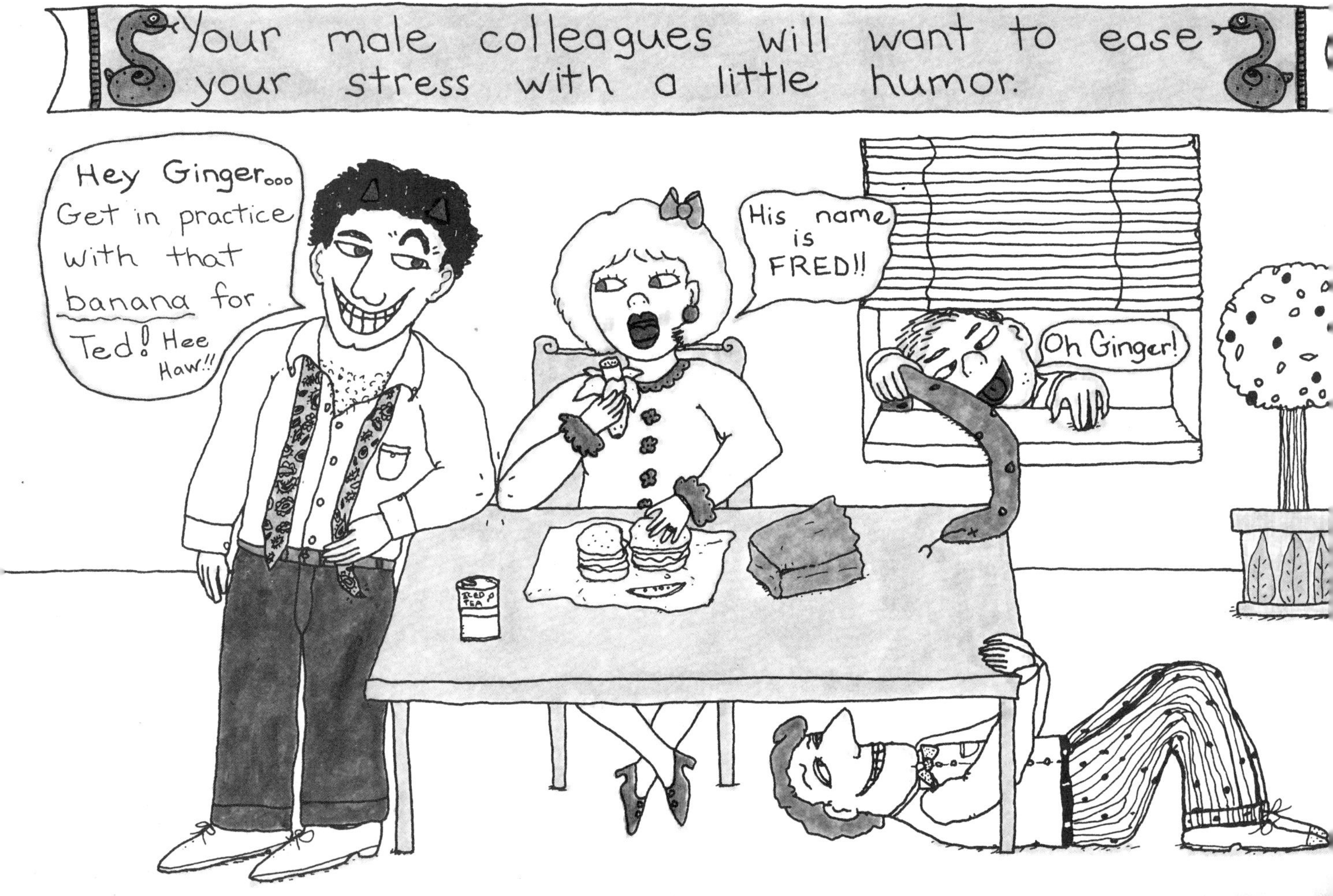

Your male colleagues will want to ease your stress with a little humor.
Hey Ginger... Get in practice with that banana for Ted! Hee Haw!!
His name is FRED!!
Oh Ginger!

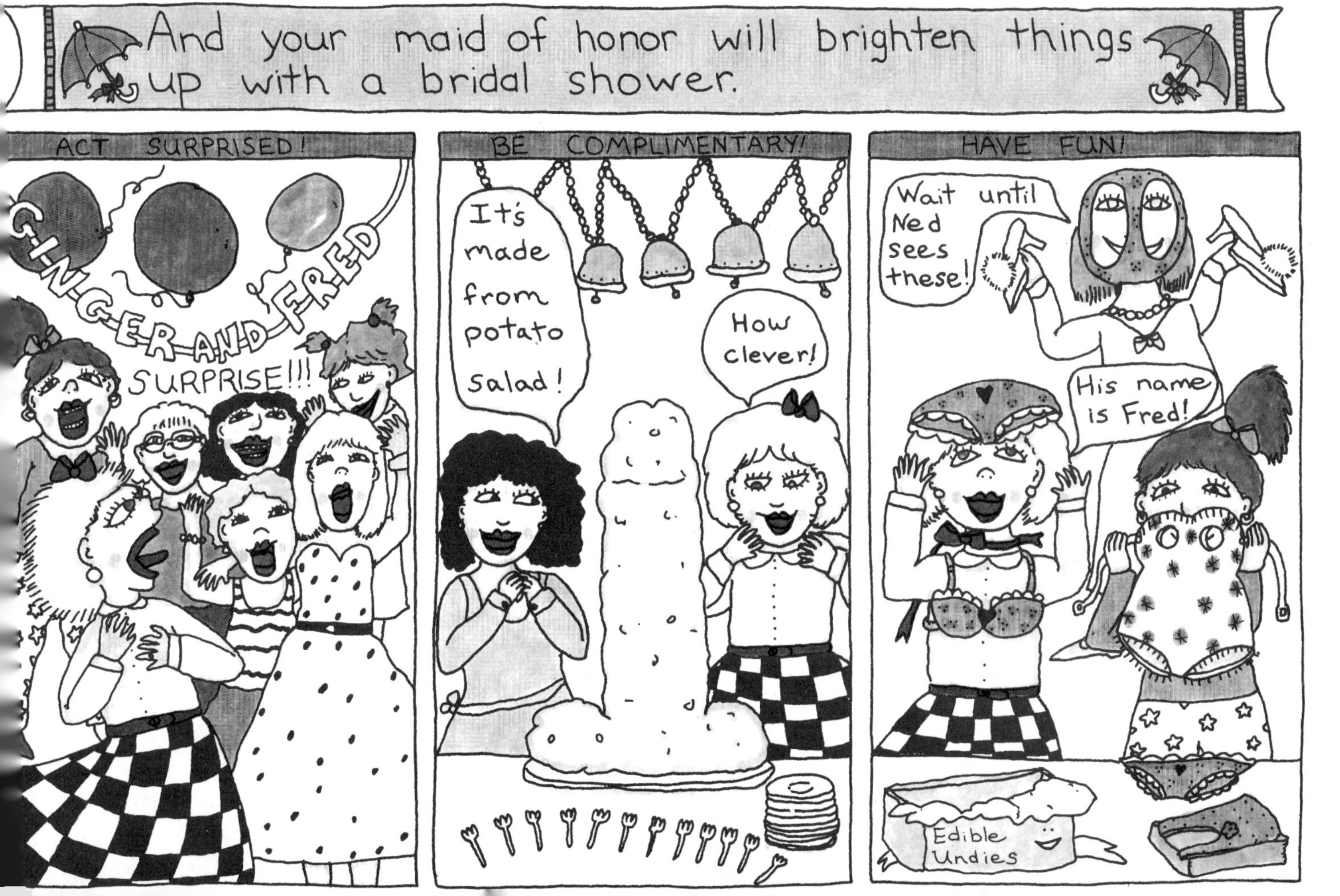

And your maid of honor will brighten things up with a bridal shower.
ACT SURPRISED!
GINGER AND FRED
SURPRISE!!!
BE COMPLIMENTARY!
It's made from potato salad!
How clever!
HAVE FUN!
Wait until Ned sees these!
His name is Fred!
Edible Undies

As the wedding day draws closer, take a good, hard look in the mirror. Is the face that looks back at you the one you want to see in your wedding photos?

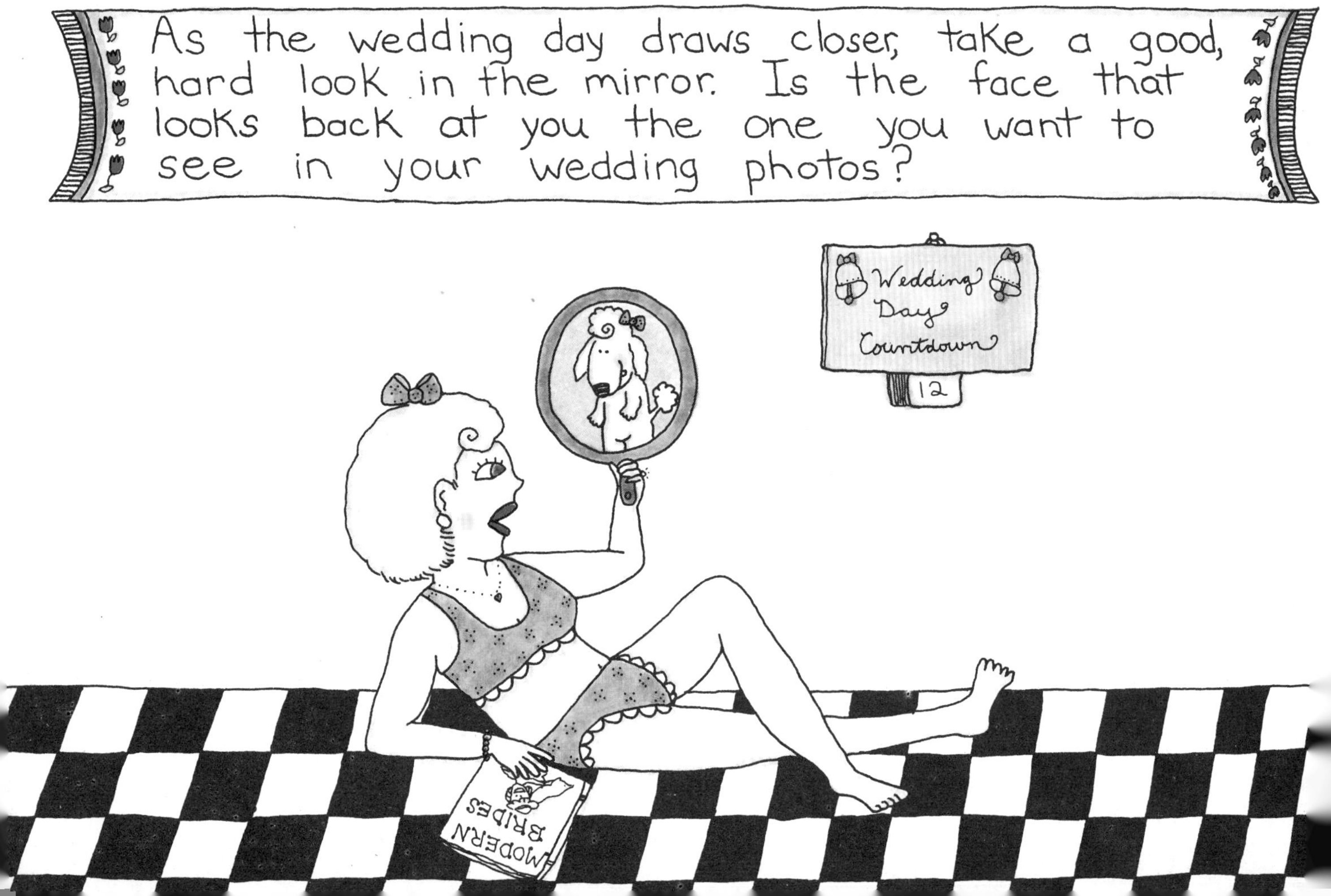
Wedding Day Countdown
12
MODERN BRIDES

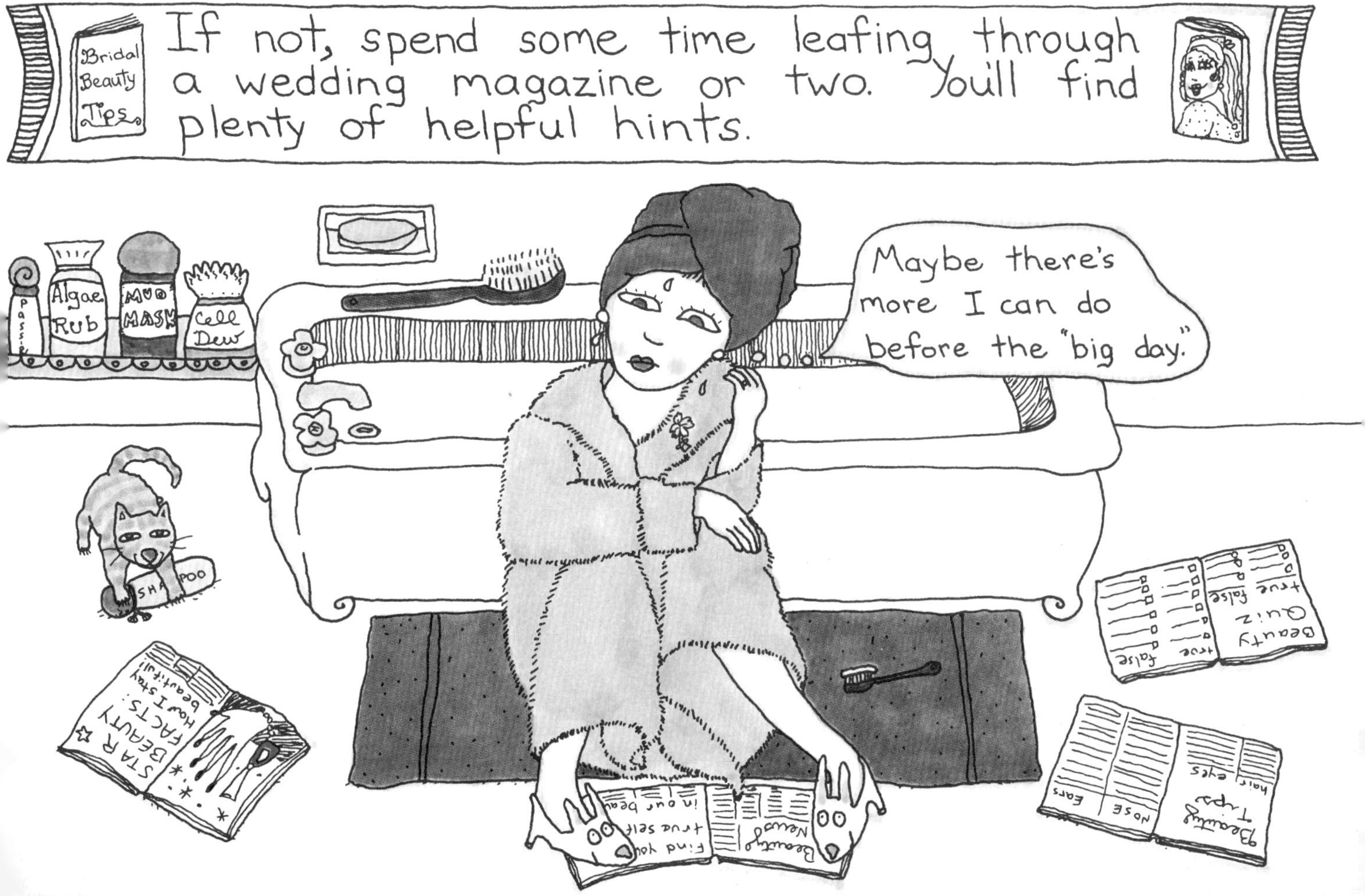
If not, spend some time leafing through a wedding magazine or two. You'll find plenty of helpful hints.
Bridal Beauty Tips
Maybe there's more I can do before the "big day."
Algae Rub
MUD MASK
Cell Dew
SHA POO
STAR BEAUTY FACTS: How I stay beautiful
Beauty Quiz
true false
Beauty Tips
hair eyes
NOSE
Ears
Beauty News
Find you true self in our beau

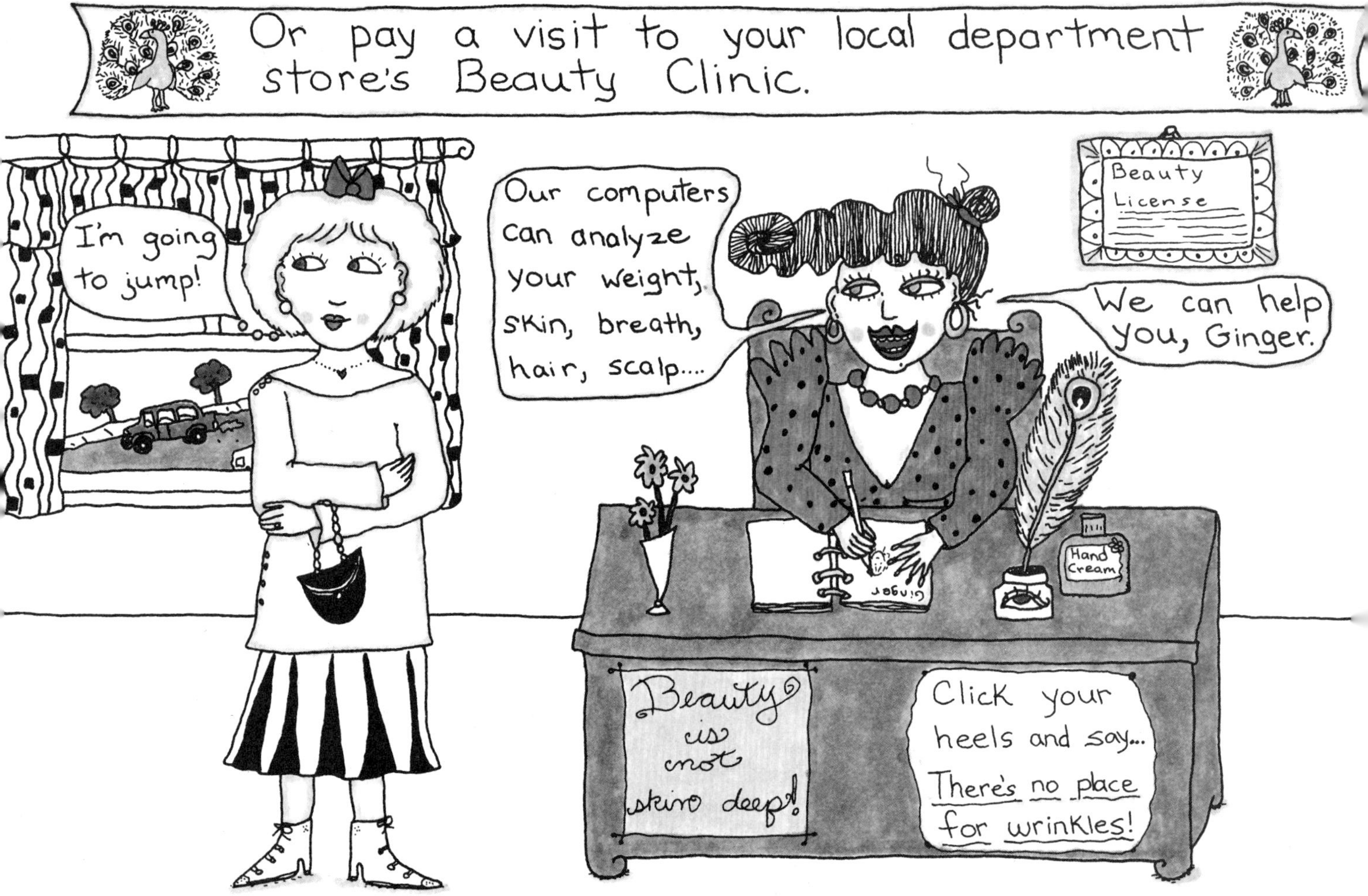

Or pay a visit to your local department store's Beauty Clinic.
I'm going to jump!
Our computers can analyze your weight, skin, breath, hair, scalp....
We can help you, Ginger.
Beauty License
Ginger
Hand Cream
Beauty is not skin deep!
Click your heels and say... There's no place for wrinkles!

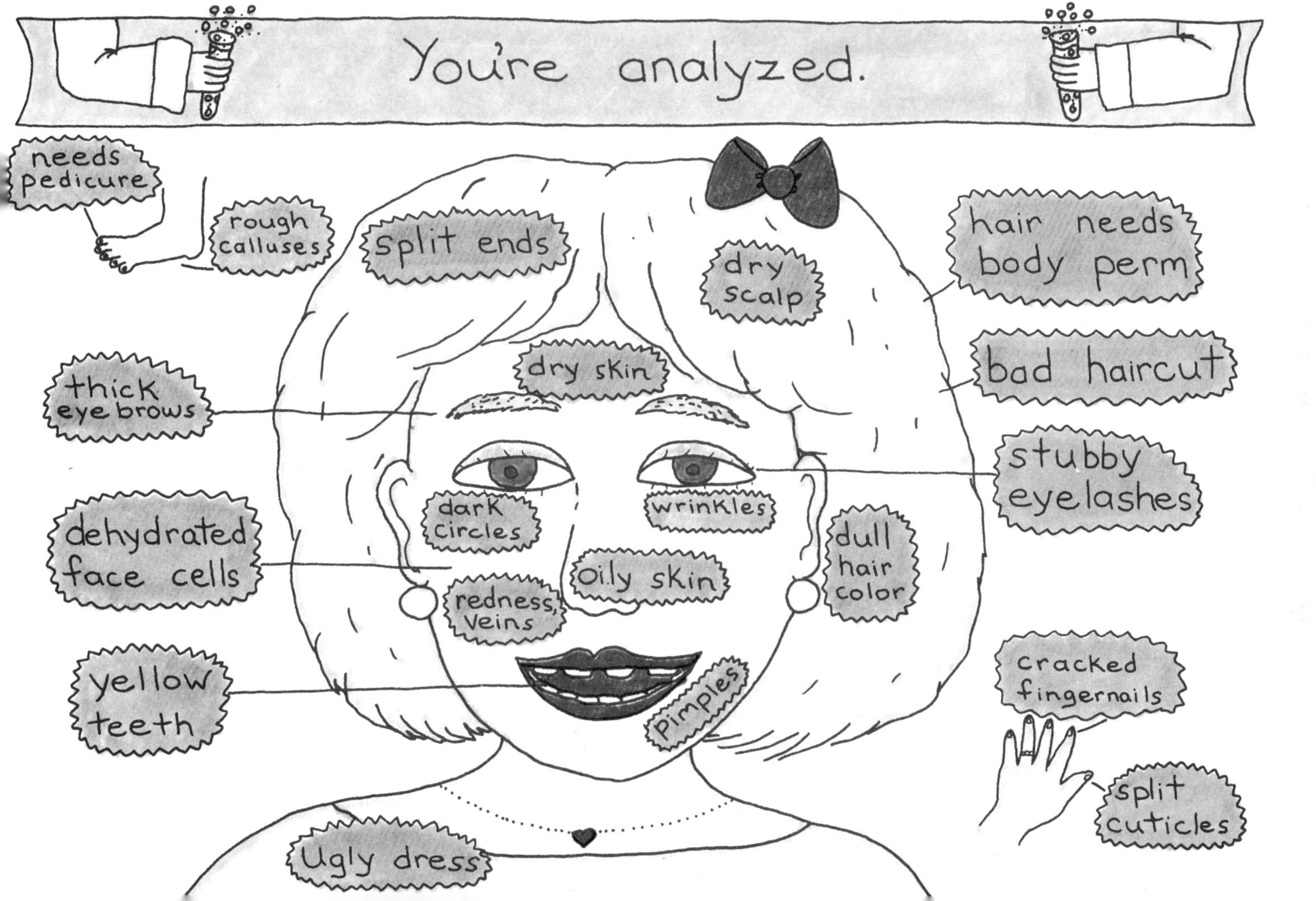
You're analyzed.
needs pedicure
rough calluses
split ends
dry scalp
hair needs body perm
dry skin
thick eye brows
bad haircut
stubby eyelashes
dark circles
wrinkles
dehydrated face cells
oily skin
dull hair color
redness, veins
yellow teeth
pimples
cracked fingernails
split cuticles
Ugly dress

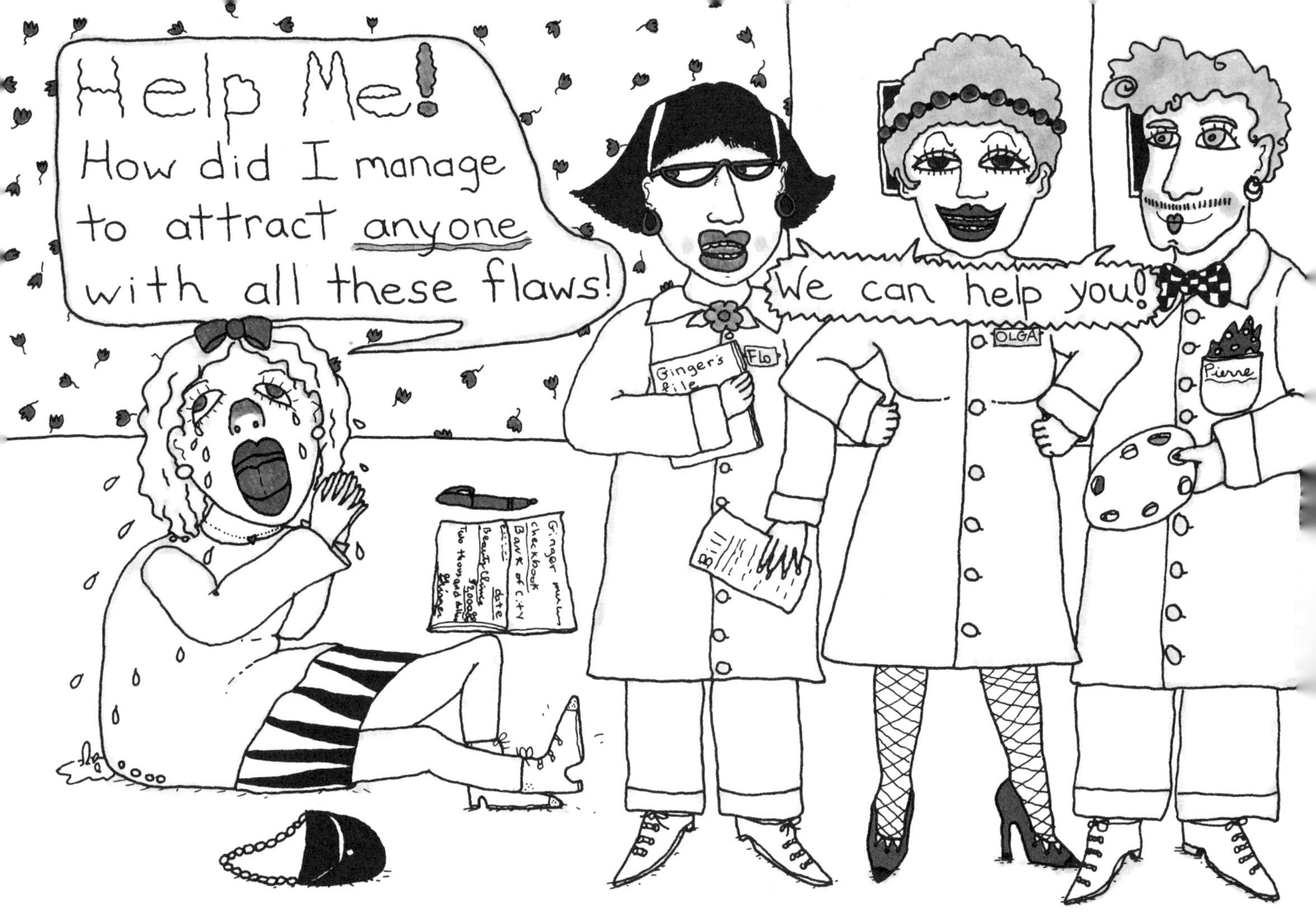
Help Me!
How did I manage to attract anyone with all these flaws!
We can help you!
Ginger's file
Flo
OLGA
Pierre
Bill
Ginger
checkbook
Bank of City
date
Beauty Clinic
$2000.00
Two thousand dollars

The treatment begins.
The Miracle
The Miracle
Facial
Haircut
Massage
Vegetable Peel
Scalp treatment
Hair cellophane
Wax legs, armpits
Pedicure
Full manicure
Eyebrows tweezed
Hair body perm
Polish teeth

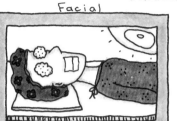

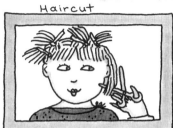

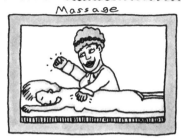

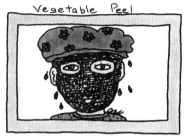

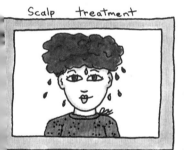

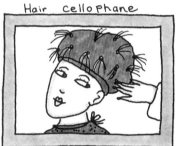

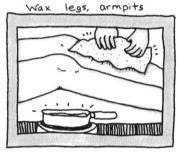

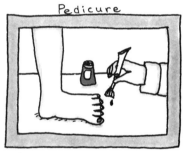

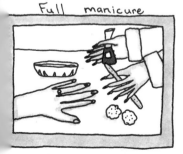

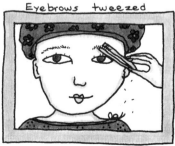

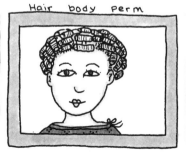

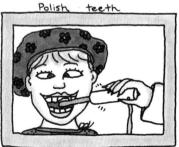

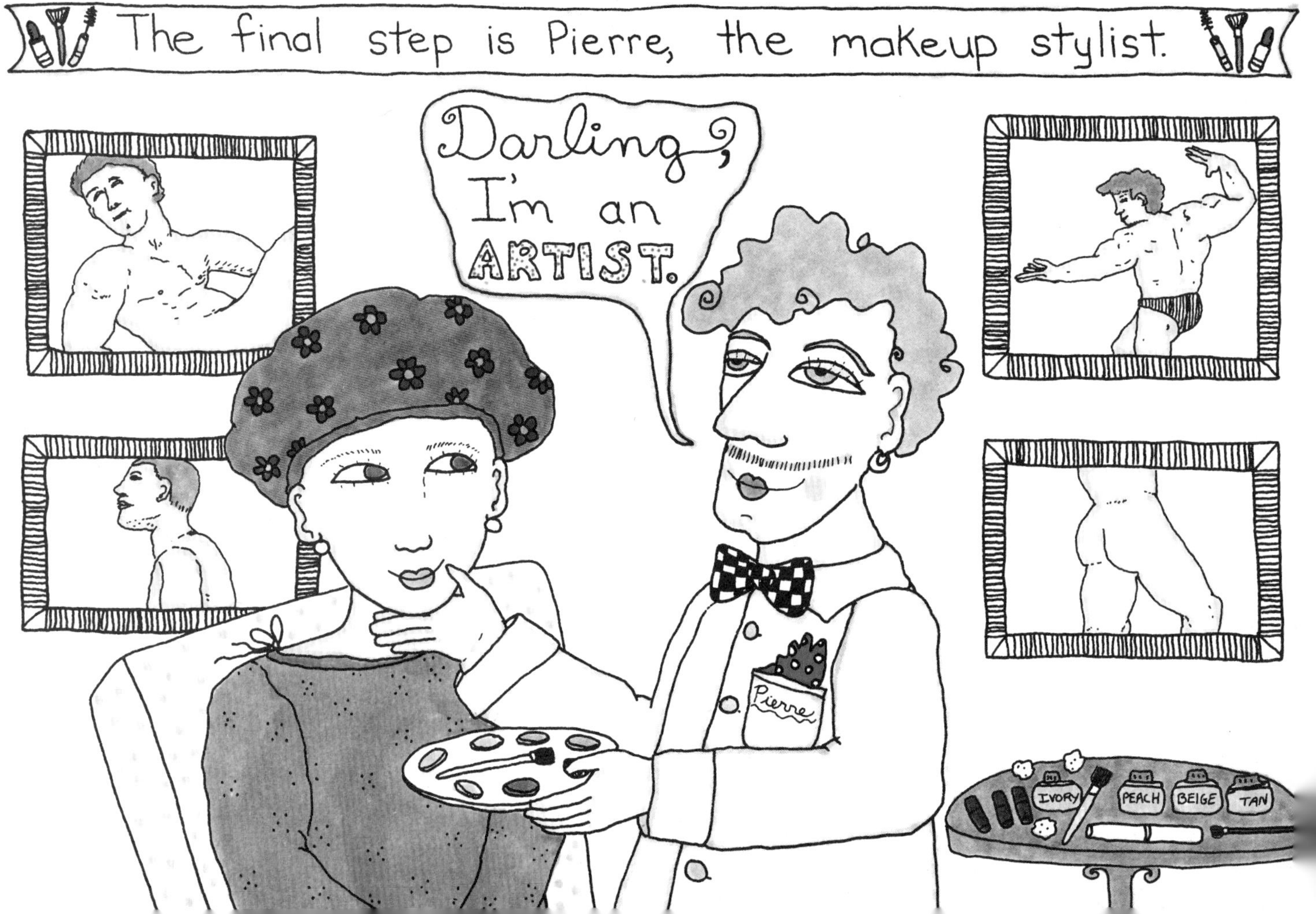
The final step is Pierre, the makeup stylist.
Darling, I'm an ARTIST.
Pierre
IVORY
PEACH
BEIGE
TAN

At last, you can show off your new look.

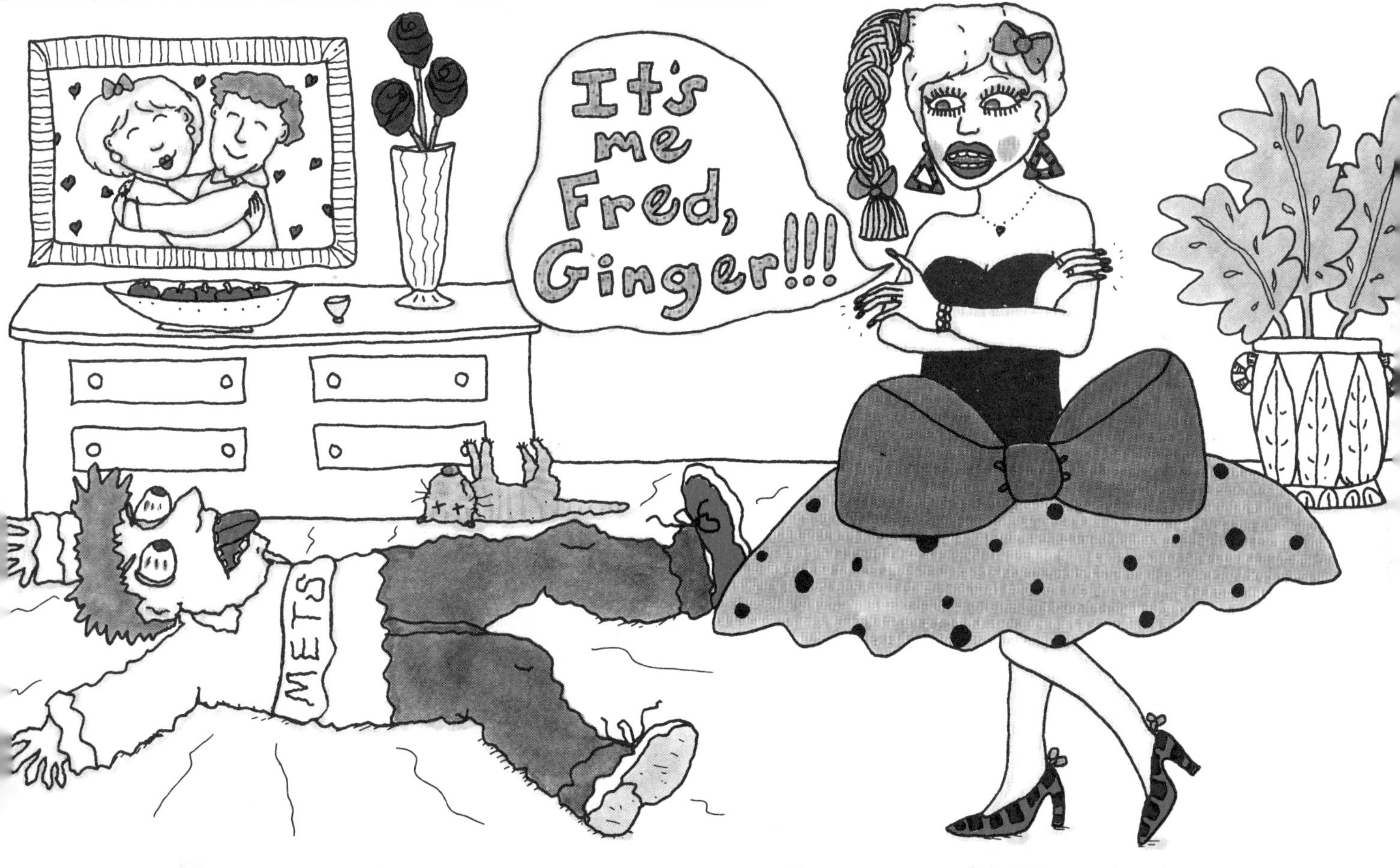
It's me Fred, Ginger!!!
METS

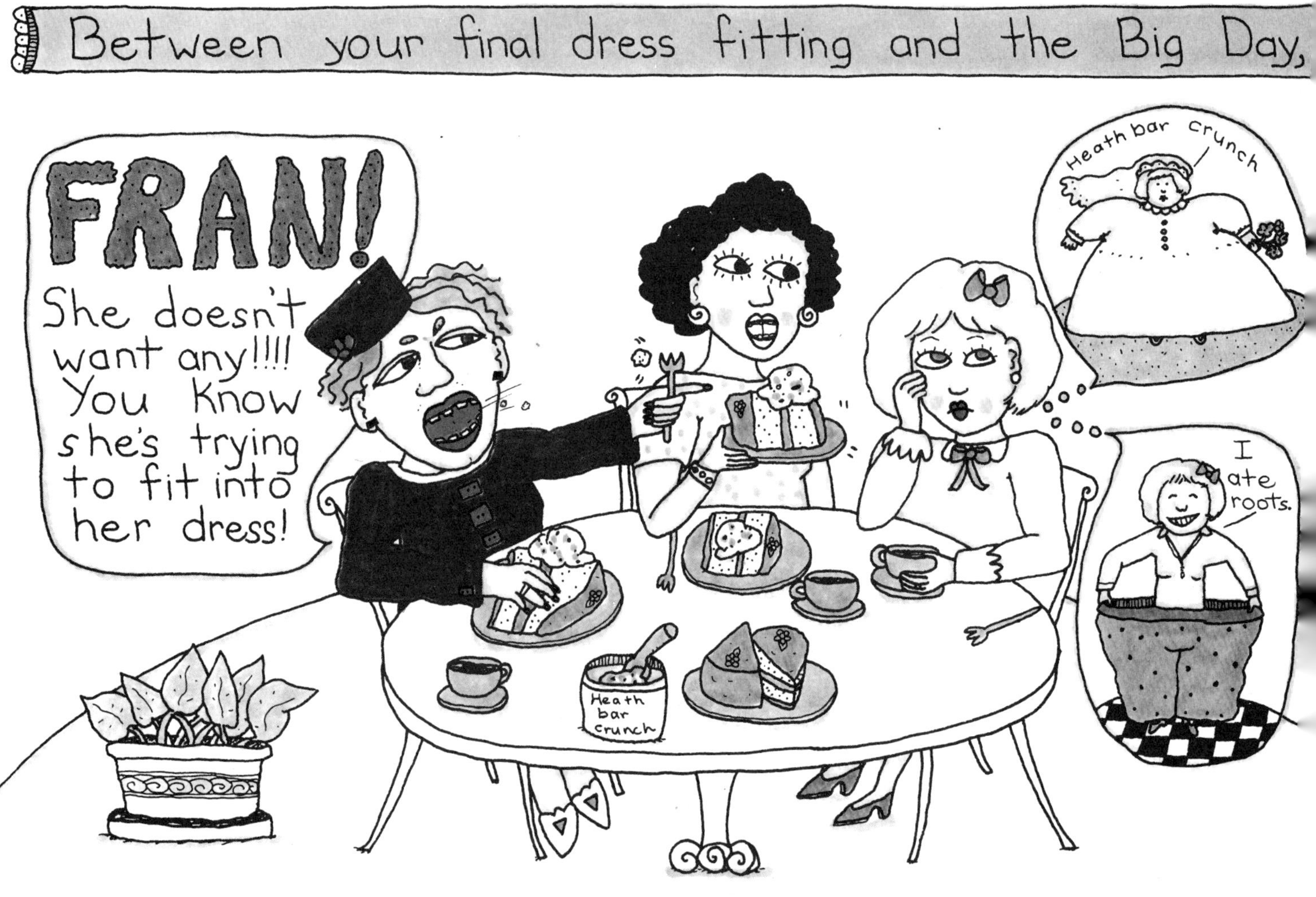

Between your final dress fitting and the Big Day,
FRAN!
She doesn't want any!!!! You Know she's trying to fit into her dress!
Heath bar crunch
I ate roots.
Heath bar crunch

Keep a close watch on your weight.

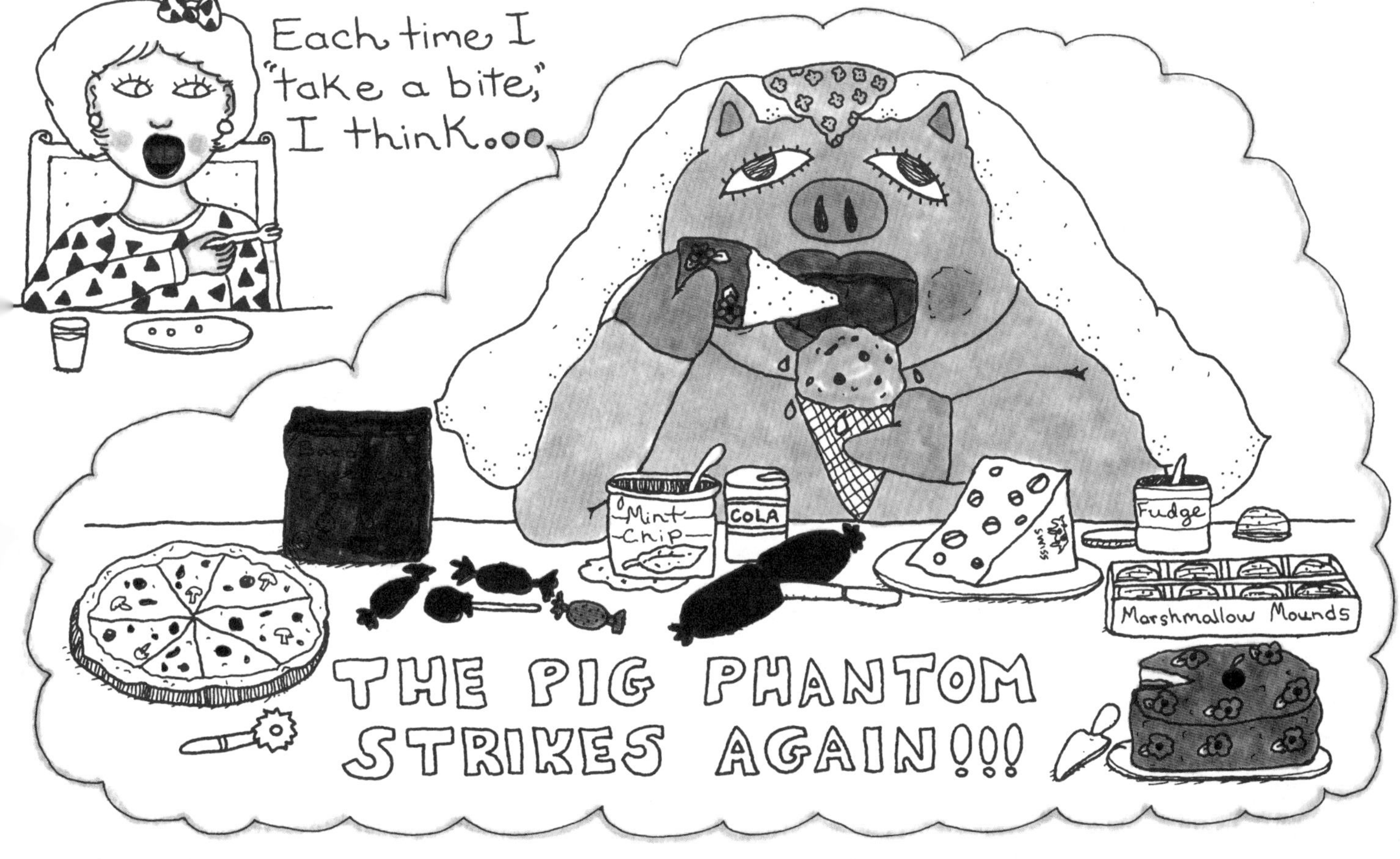
Each time I "take a bite," I think...
Mint Chip
COLA
SWISS
Fudge
Marshmallow Mounds
THE PIG PHANTOM STRIKES AGAIN!!!

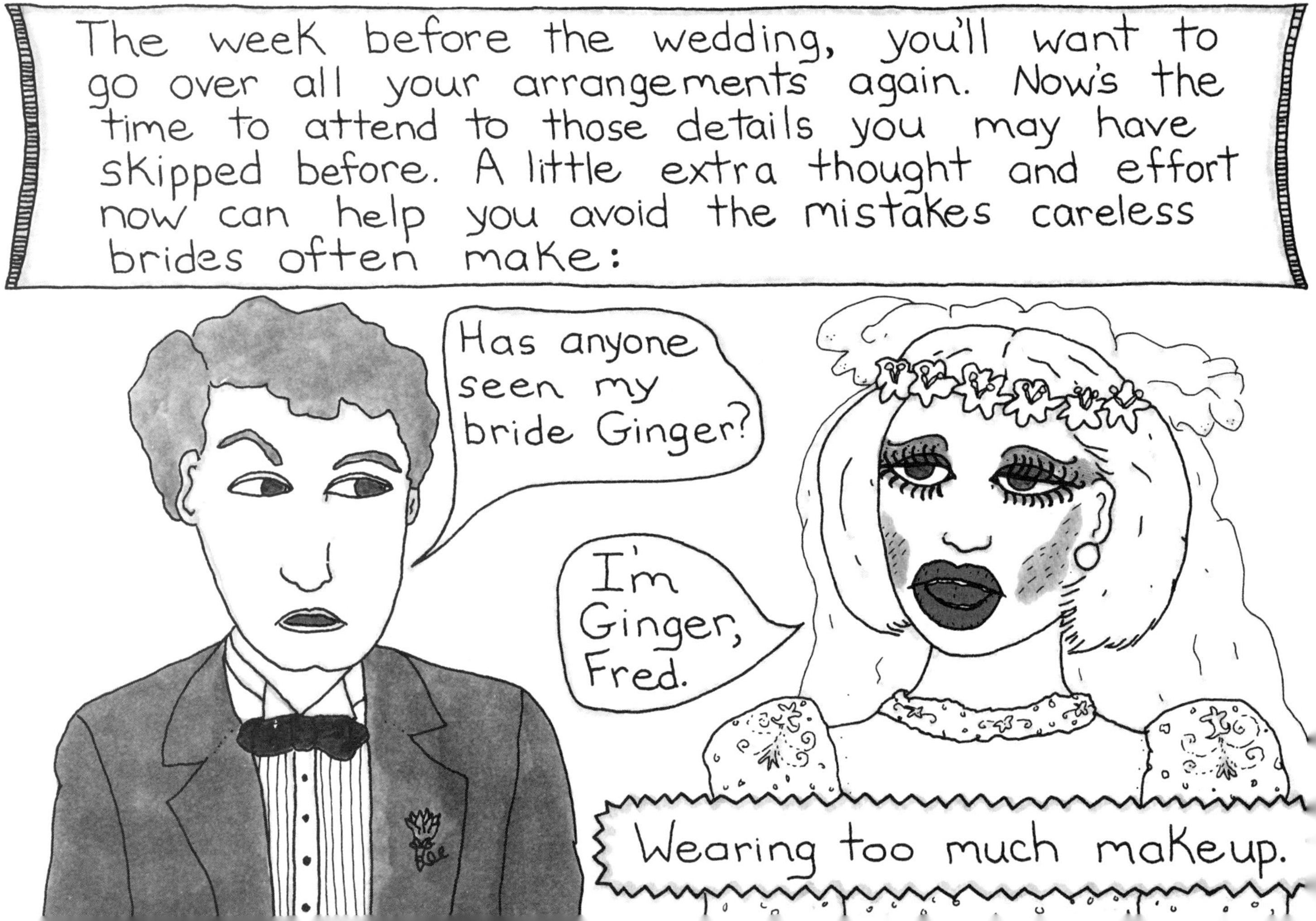
The week before the wedding, you'll want to go over all your arrangements again. Now's the time to attend to those details you may have skipped before. A little extra thought and effort now can help you avoid the mistakes careless brides often make:
Has anyone seen my bride Ginger?
I'm Ginger, Fred.
Wearing too much makeup.

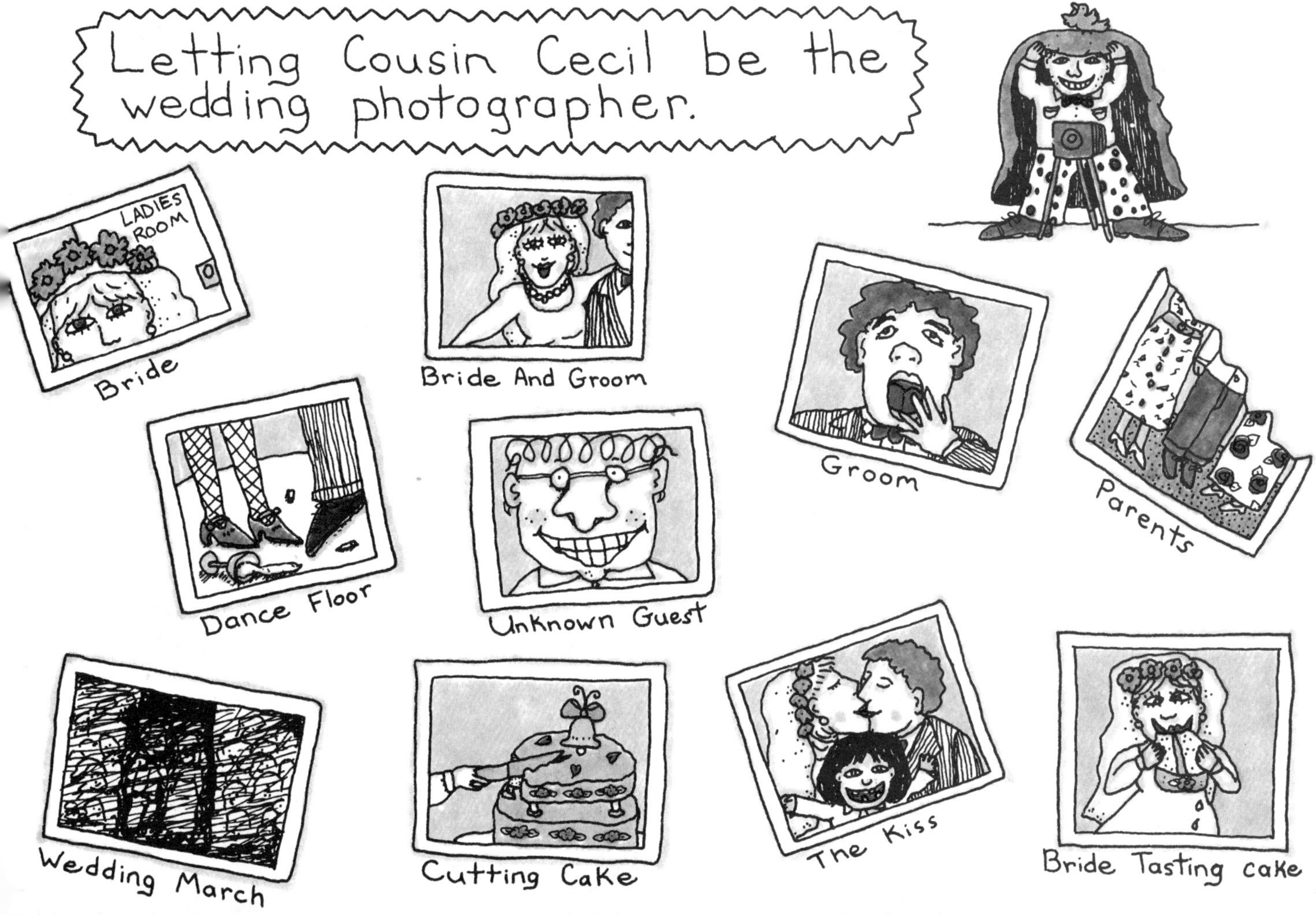
Letting Cousin Cecil be the wedding photographer.
LADIES ROOM
Bride
Bride And Groom
Groom
Parents
Dance Floor
Unknown Guest
Wedding March
Cutting Cake
The Kiss
Bride Tasting cake

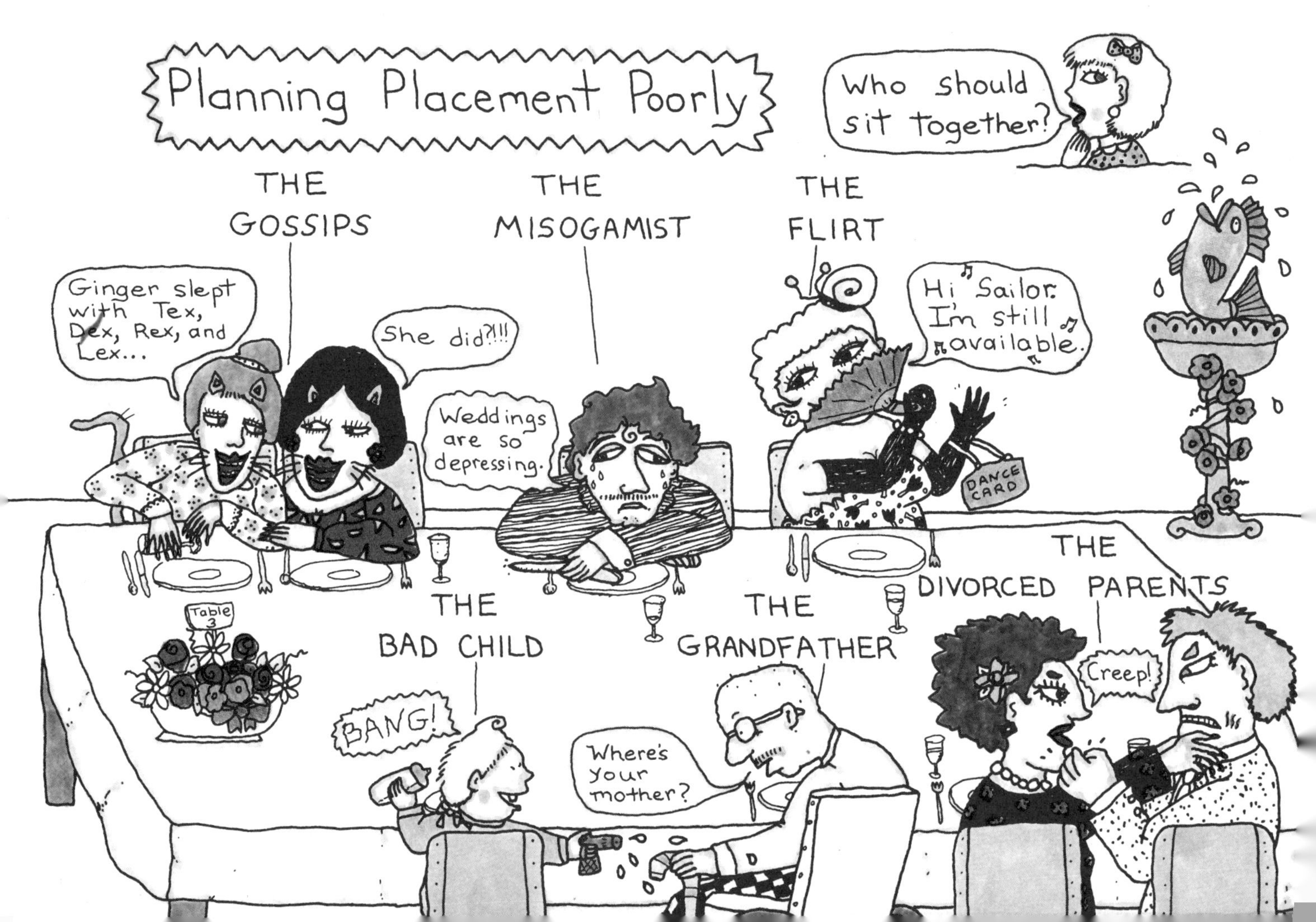
Planning Placement Poorly
Who should sit together?
THE GOSSIPS
Ginger slept with Tex, Dex, Rex, and Lex...
She did?!!!
THE MISOGAMIST
Weddings are so depressing.
THE FLIRT
Hi Sailor. I'm still available.
DANCE CARD
Table 3
THE DIVORCED PARENTS
Creep!
THE BAD CHILD
BANG!
THE GRANDFATHER
Where's your mother?

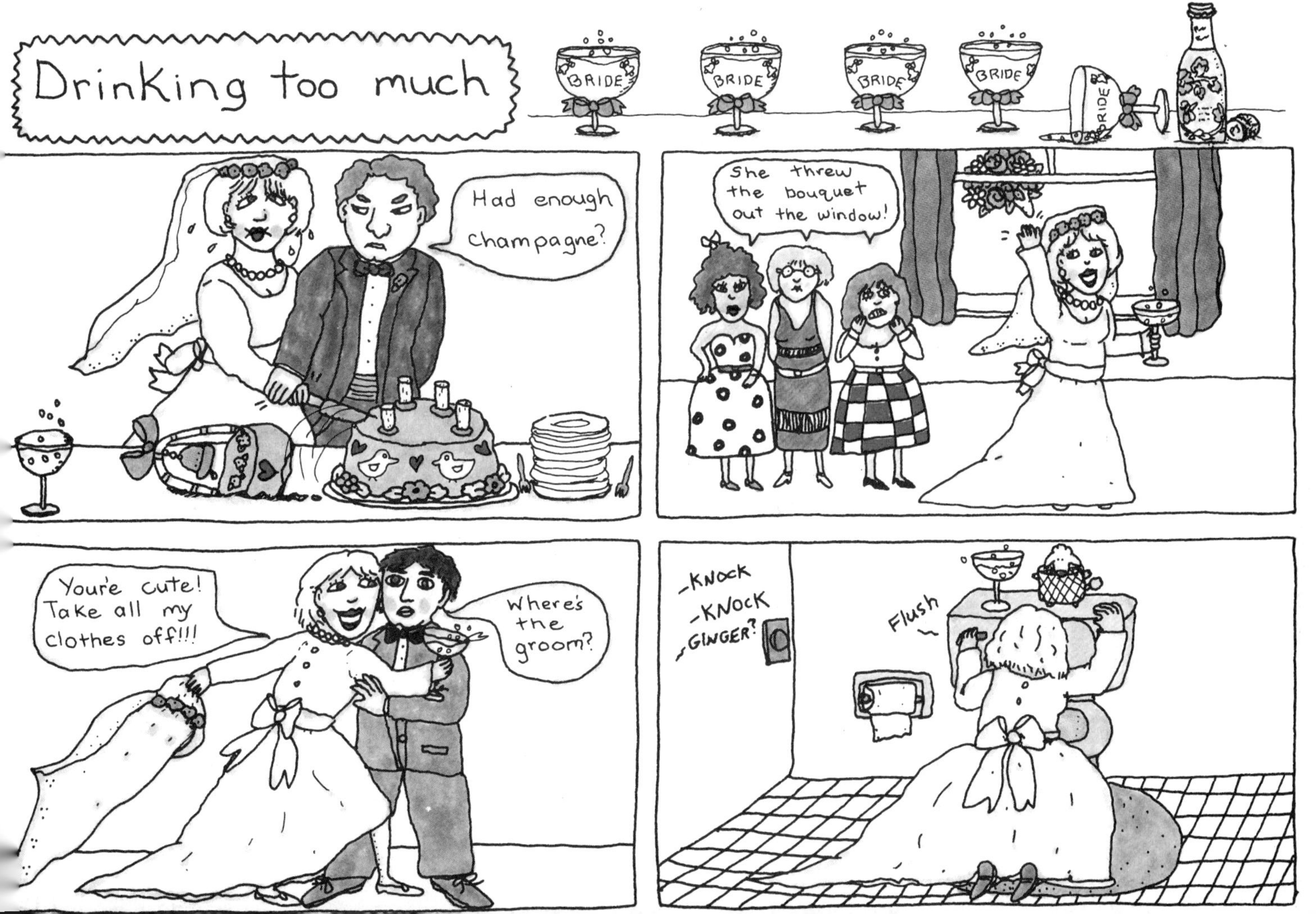
Drinking too much
BRIDE
BRIDE
BRIDE
BRIDE
BRIDE
Had enough champagne?
She threw the bouquet out the window!
You're cute! Take all my clothes off!!!
Where's the groom?
KNOCK
KNOCK
GINGER?
Flush

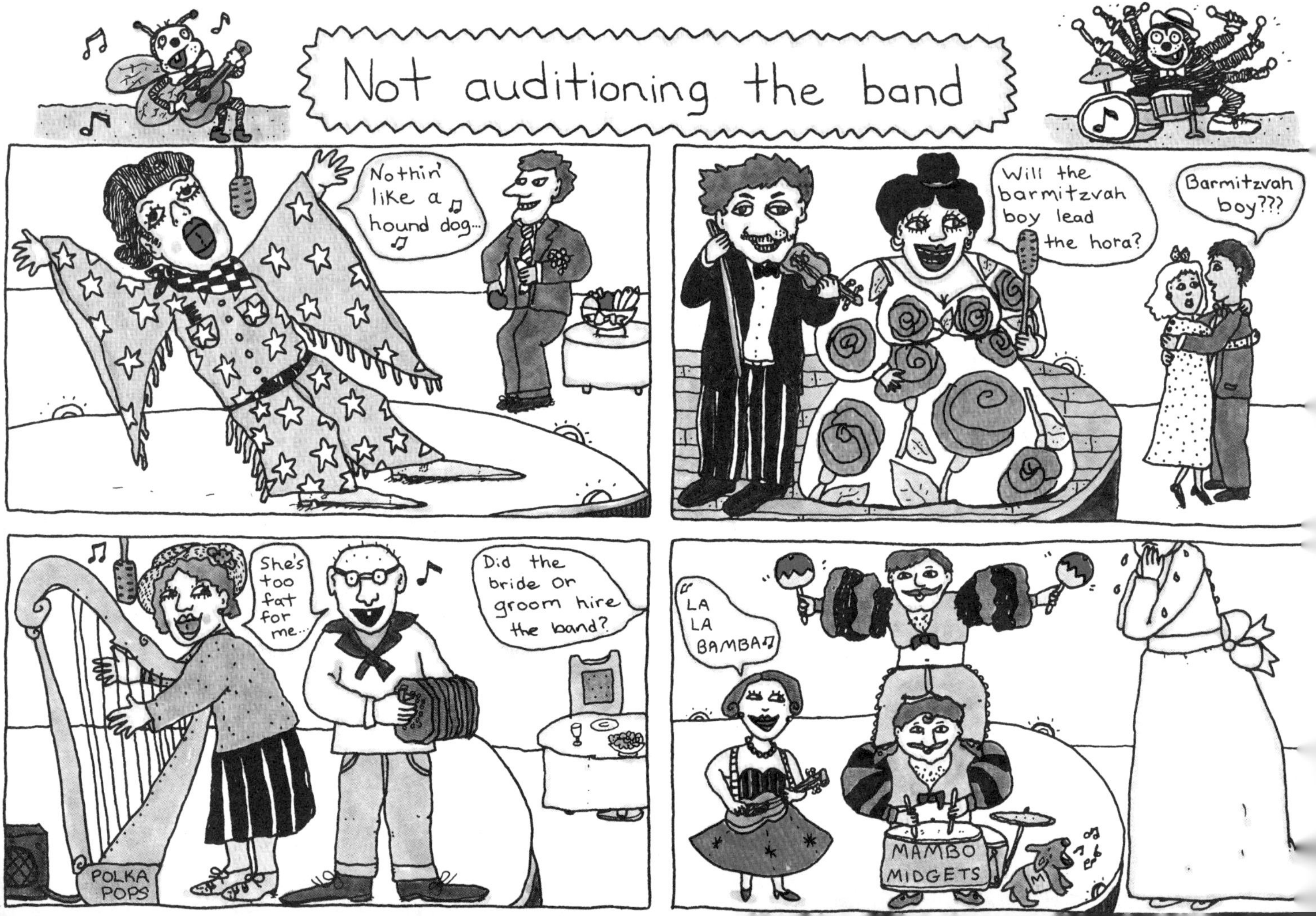
Not auditioning the band
Nothin' like a hound dog...
Will the barmitzvah boy lead the hora?
Barmitzvah boy???
She's too fat for me...
Did the bride or groom hire the band?
POLKA POPS
LA LA BAMBA
MAMBO MIDGETS

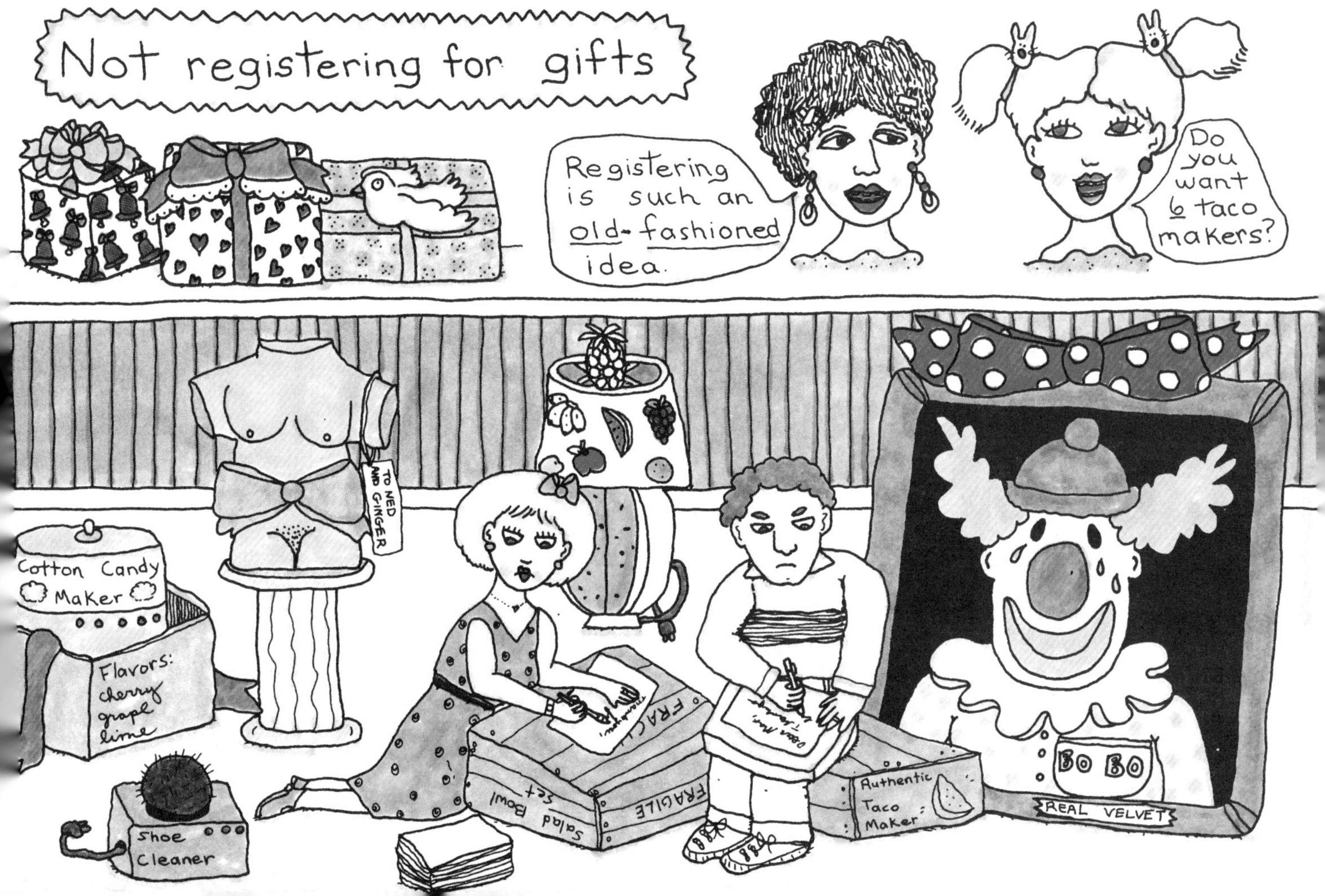
Not registering for gifts
Registering is such an old-fashioned idea.
Do you want 6 taco makers?
TO NED AND GINGER
Cotton Candy Maker
Flavors: cherry grape lime
FRAGILE
Salad Bowl set
FRAGILE
Authentic Taco Maker
BO BO
REAL VELVET
Shoe Cleaner

Many brides find this last week the most stressful time of all. Try to loosen up. Picture yourself and your new husband, already on your honeymoon.

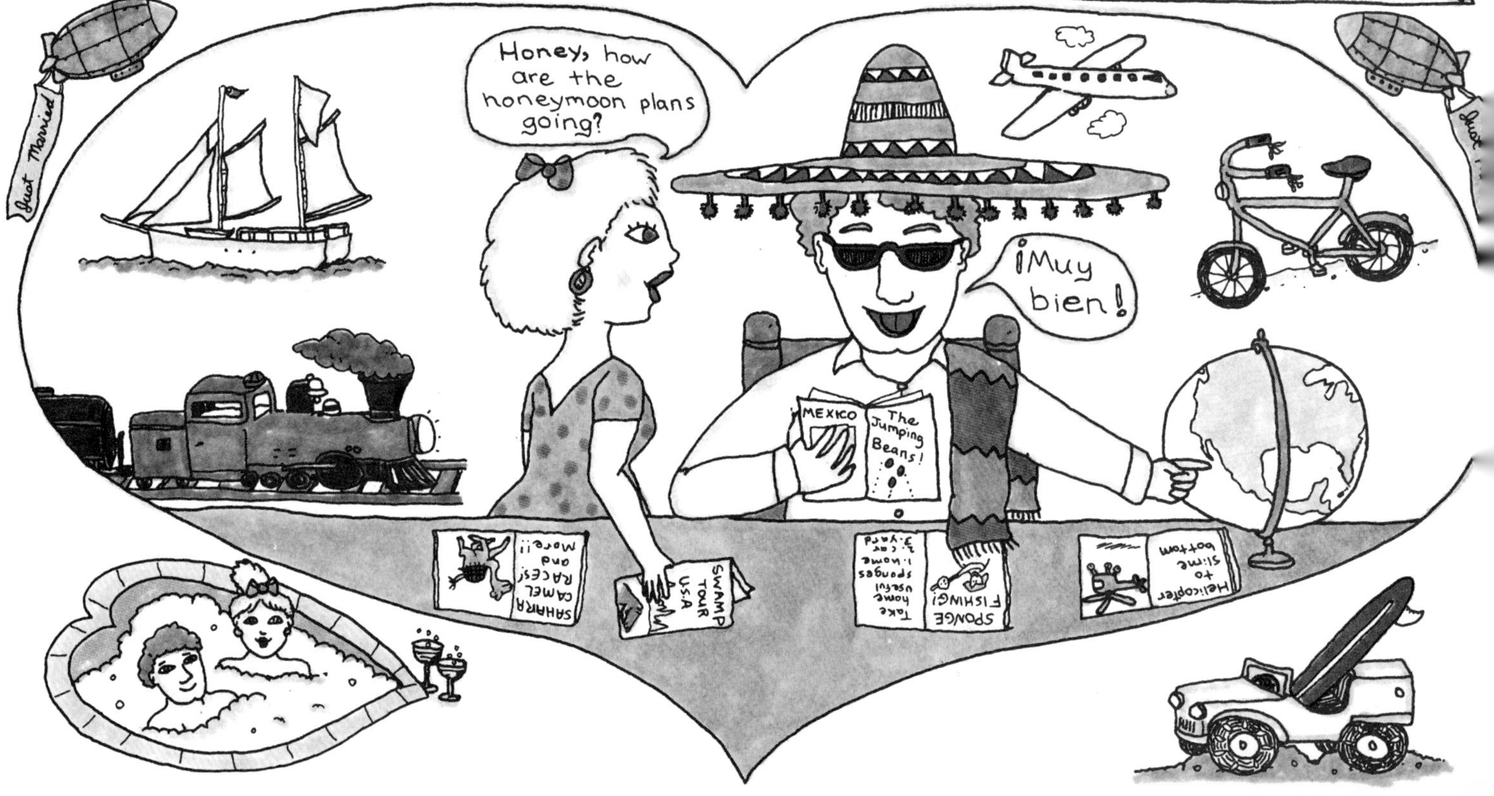

Honey, how are the honeymoon plans going?
¡Muy bien!
Just Married
Just
MEXICO
The Jumping Beans!
SWAMP TOUR U.S.A
SAHARA CAMEL RACES! and More!!
SPONGE FISHING! Take home useful sponges
Helicopter to slime bottom

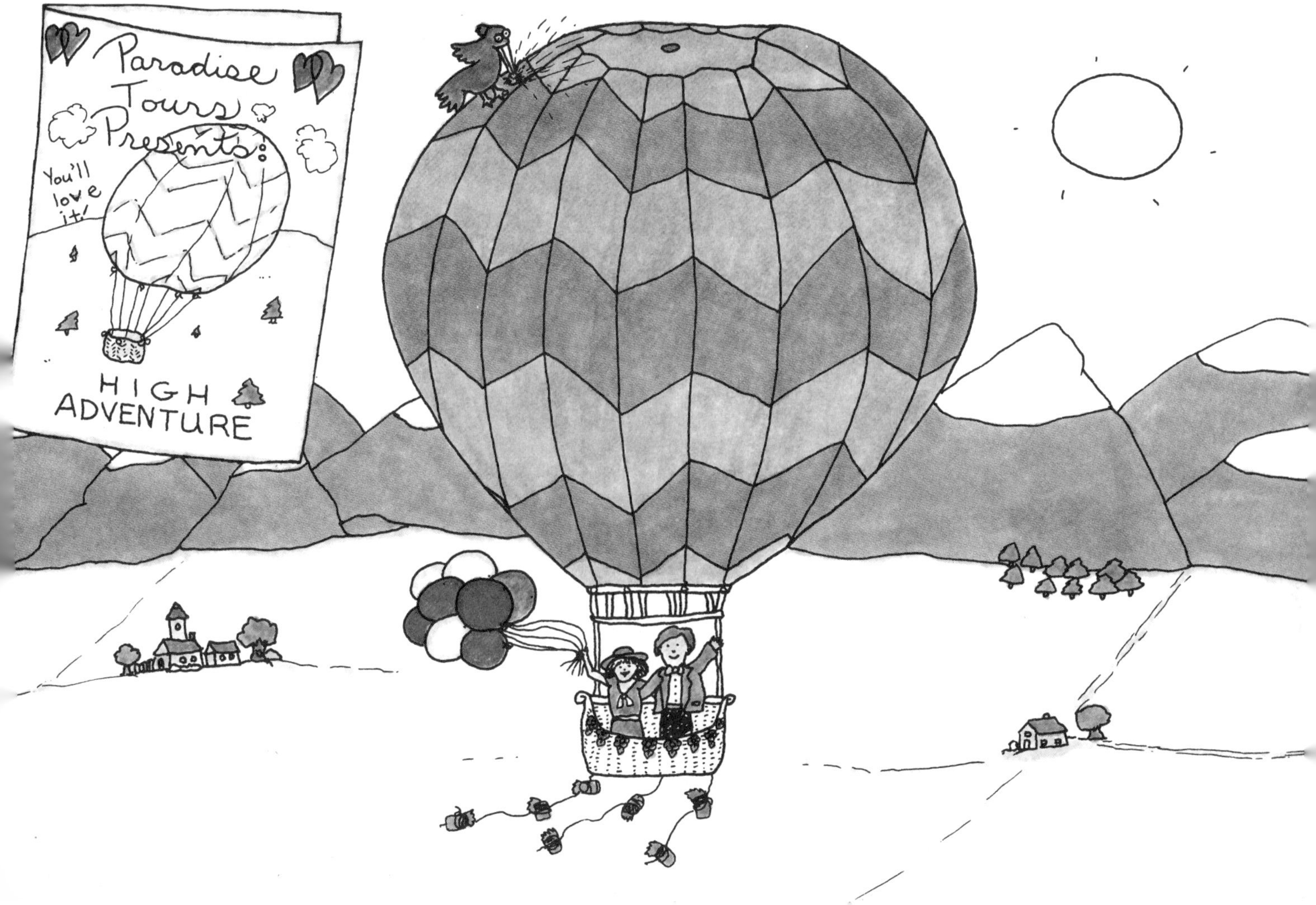
Paradise Tours Presents:
You'll love it!
HIGH ADVENTURE

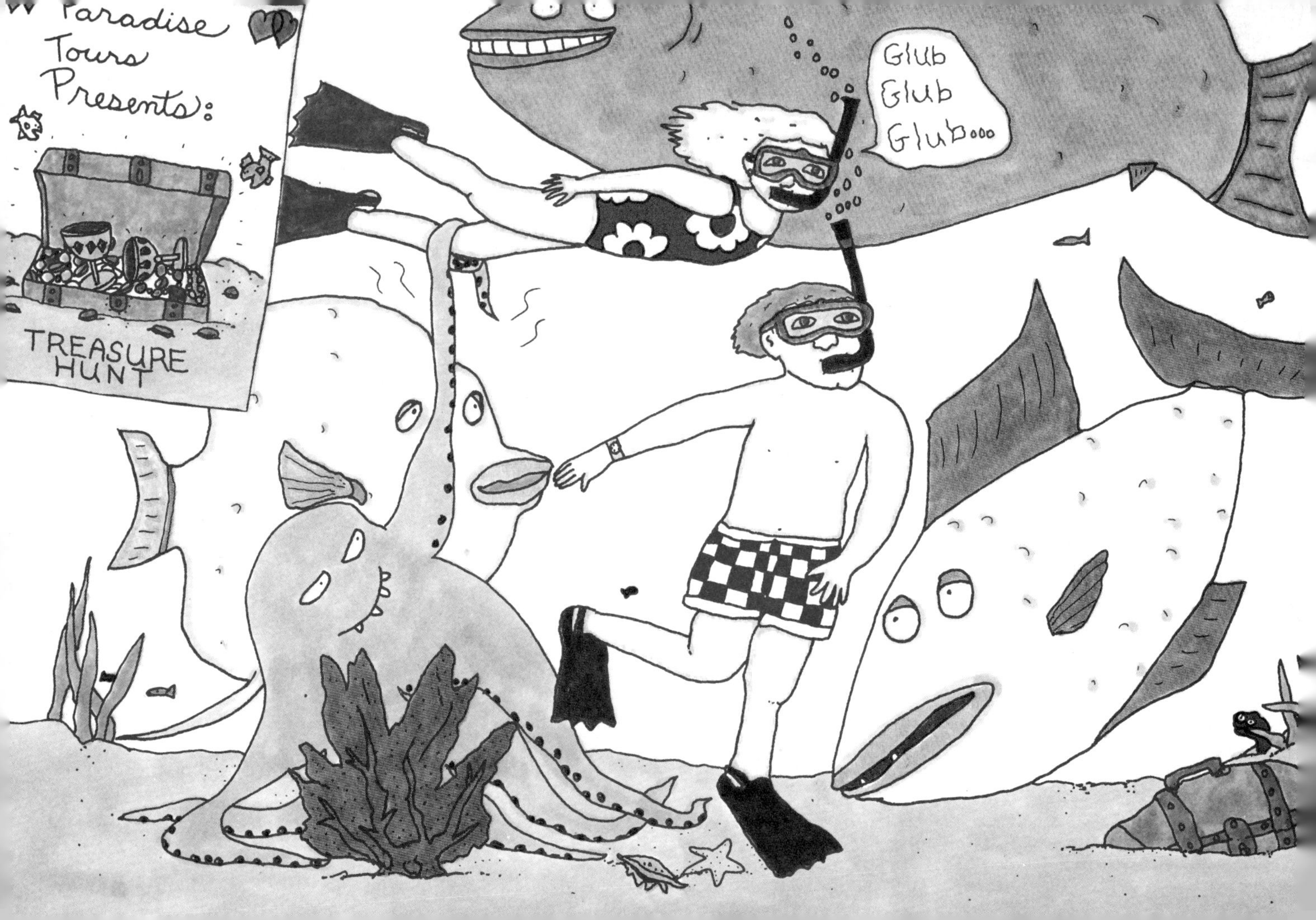
Paradise Tours Presents:
TREASURE HUNT
Glub Glub Glub...

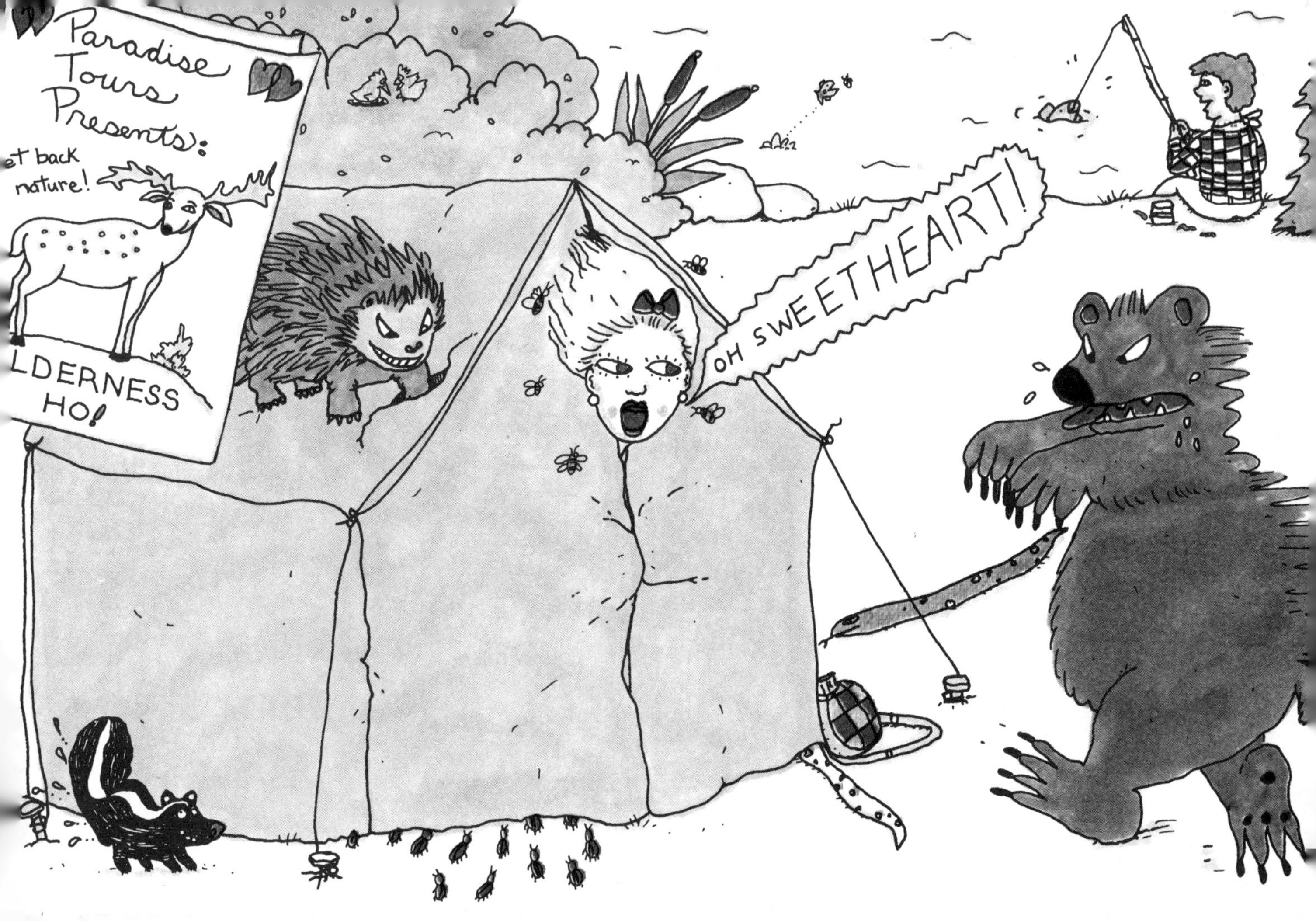
Paradise Tours Presents:
et back
nature!
LDERNESS
HO!
OH SWEETHEART!

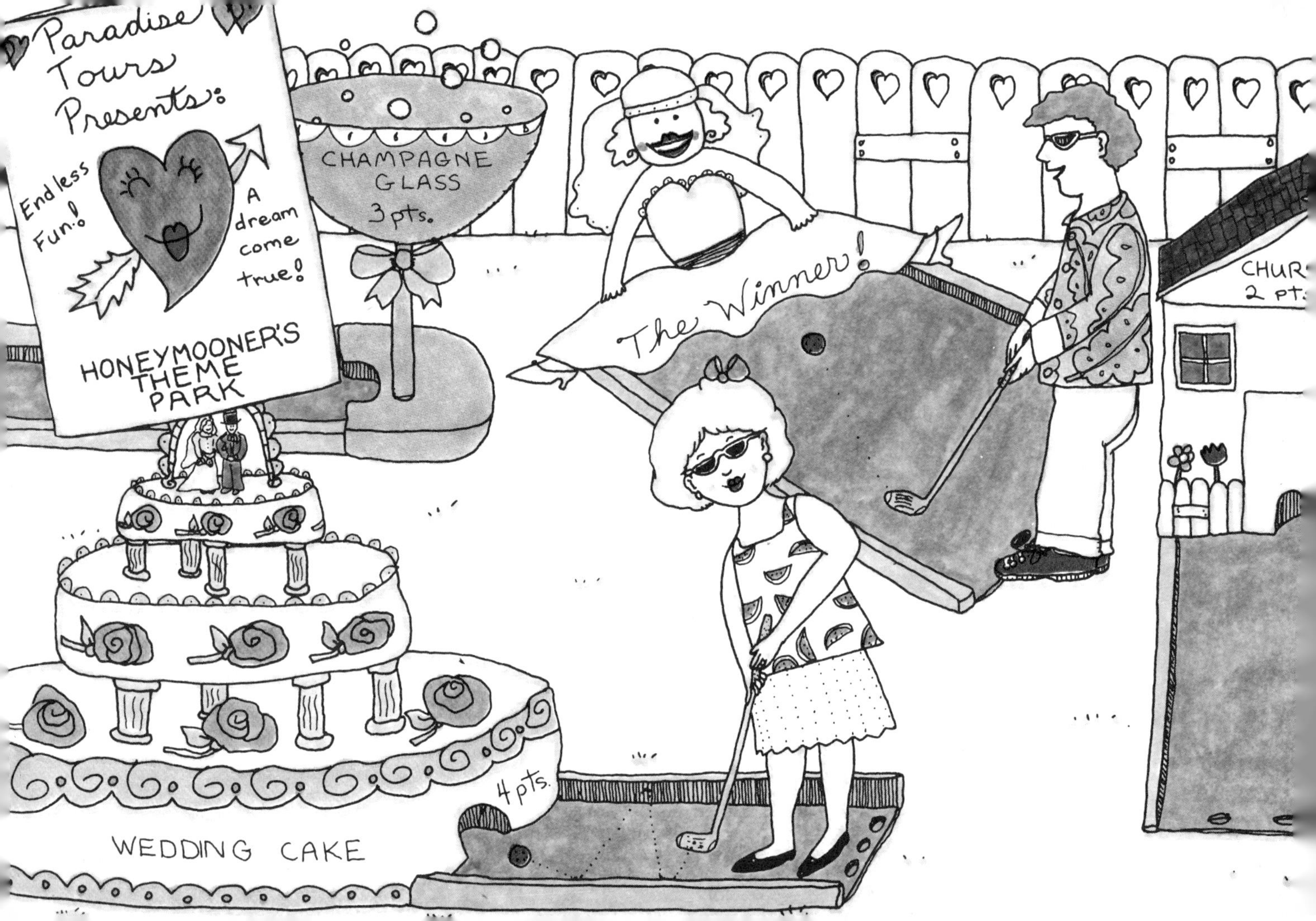
Paradise Tours Presents:
Endless Fun!
A dream come true!
HONEYMOONER'S THEME PARK
CHAMPAGNE GLASS 3 pts.
The Winner!
CHUR 2 pt
4 pts.
WEDDING CAKE

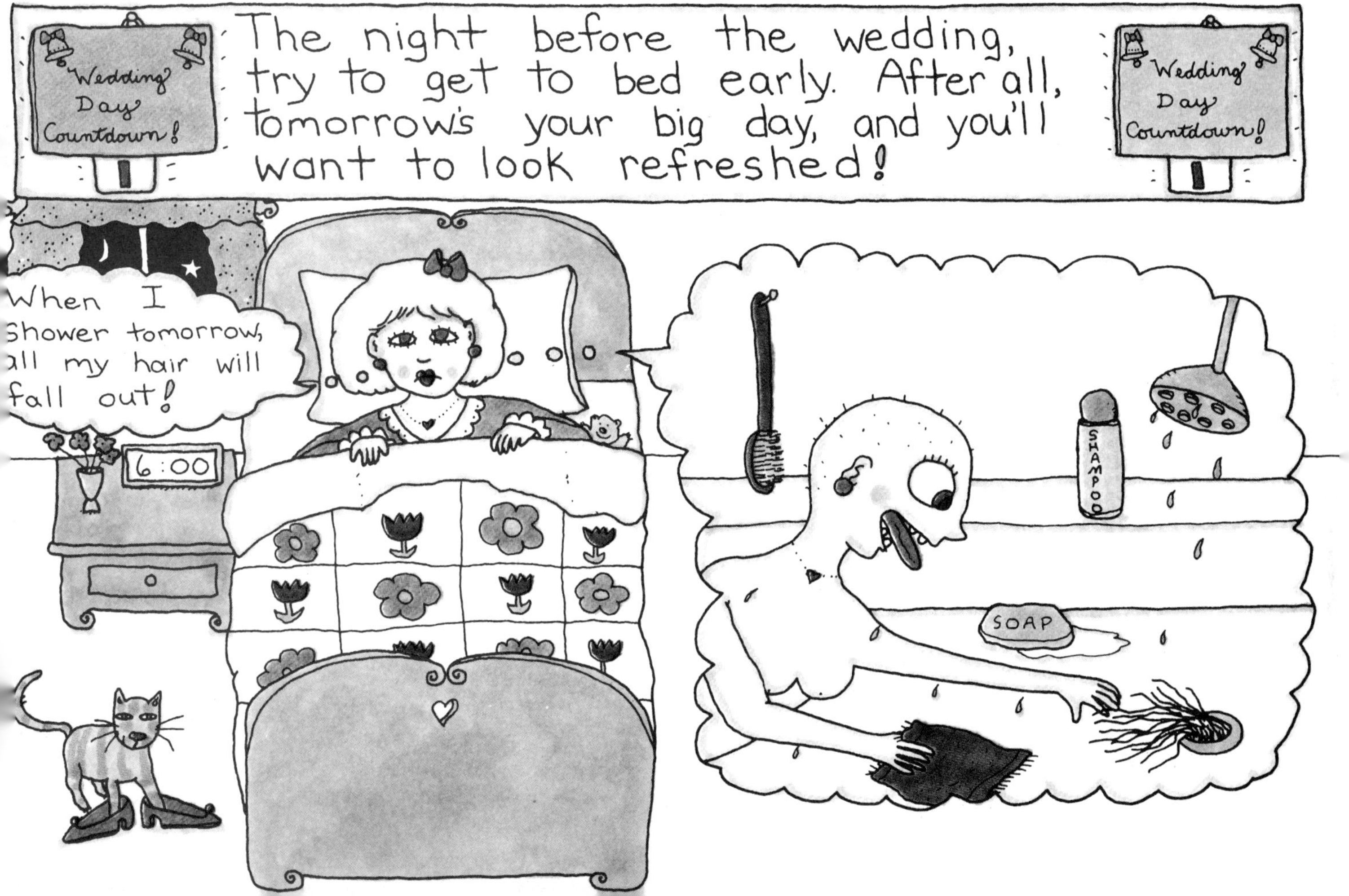
Wedding Day Countdown!
1
The night before the wedding, try to get to bed early. After all, tomorrow's your big day, and you'll want to look refreshed!
Wedding Day Countdown!
1
When I shower tomorrow, all my hair will fall out!
6:00
SHAMPOO
SOAP

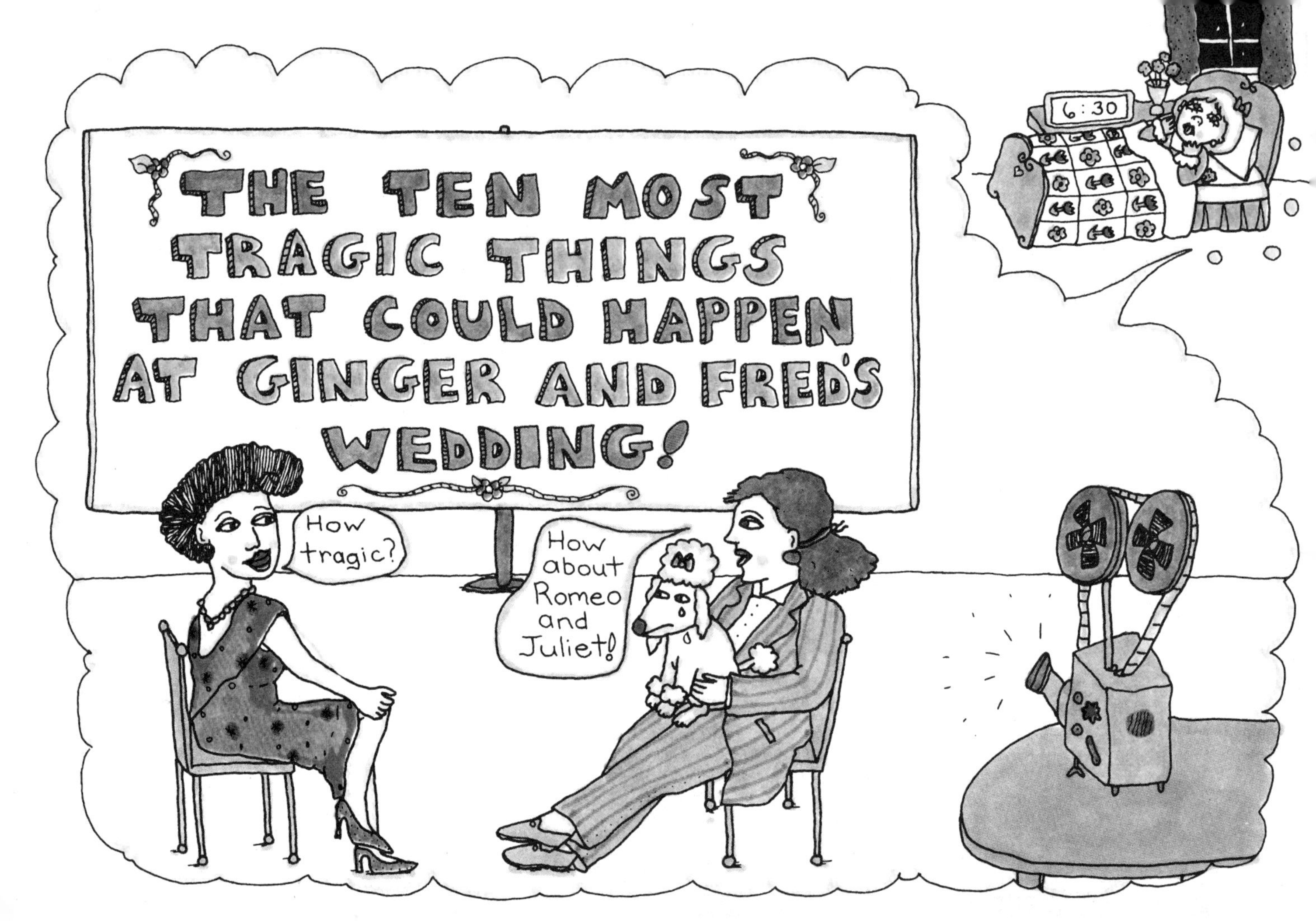
6:30
THE TEN MOST TRAGIC THINGS THAT COULD HAPPEN AT GINGER AND FRED'S WEDDING!
How tragic?
How about Romeo and Juliet!

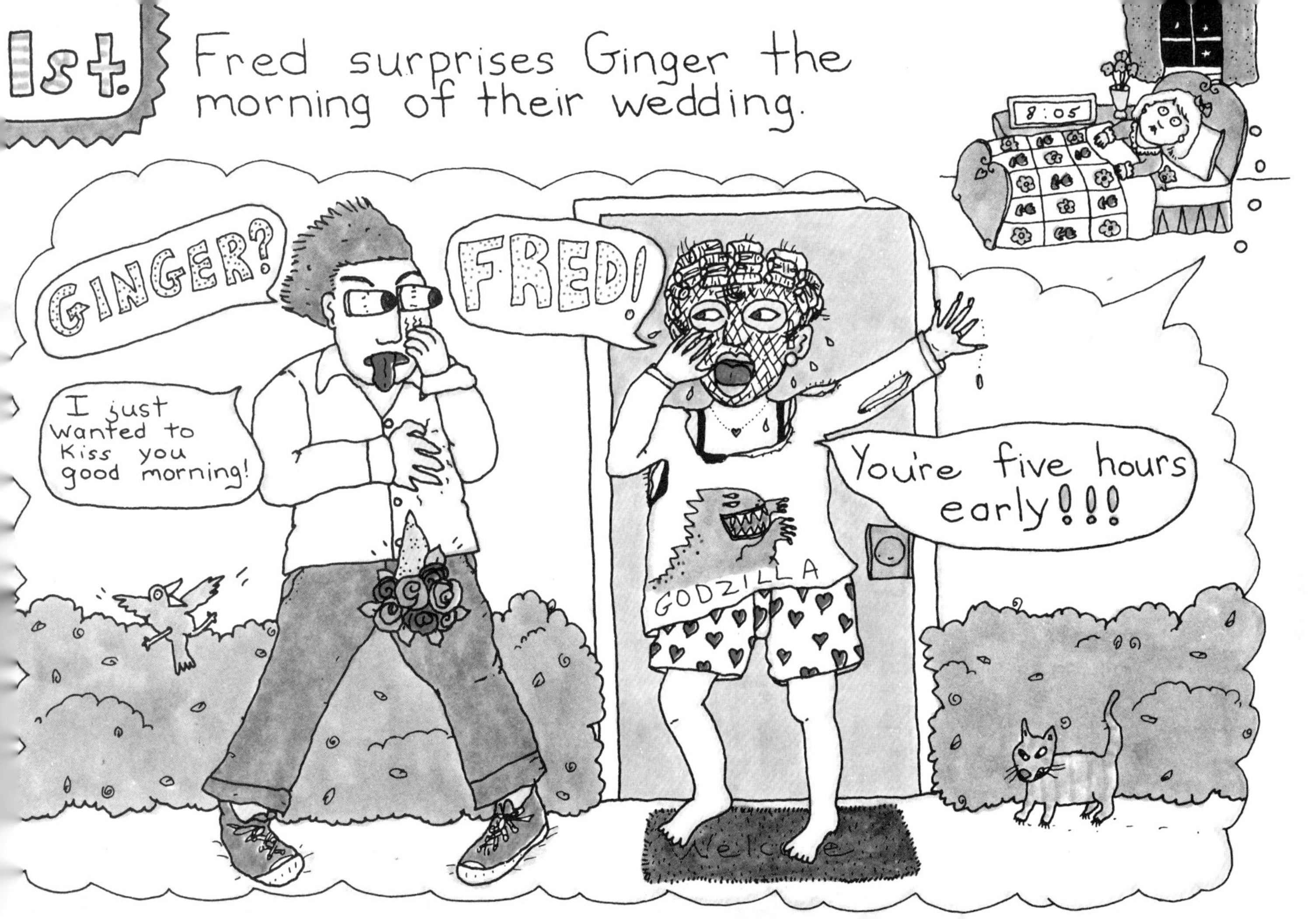
1st.
Fred surprises Ginger the morning of their wedding.
8:05
GINGER?
FRED!
I just wanted to kiss you good morning!
You're five hours early!!!
GODZILLA

2nd. Mother wears white with rhinestones.

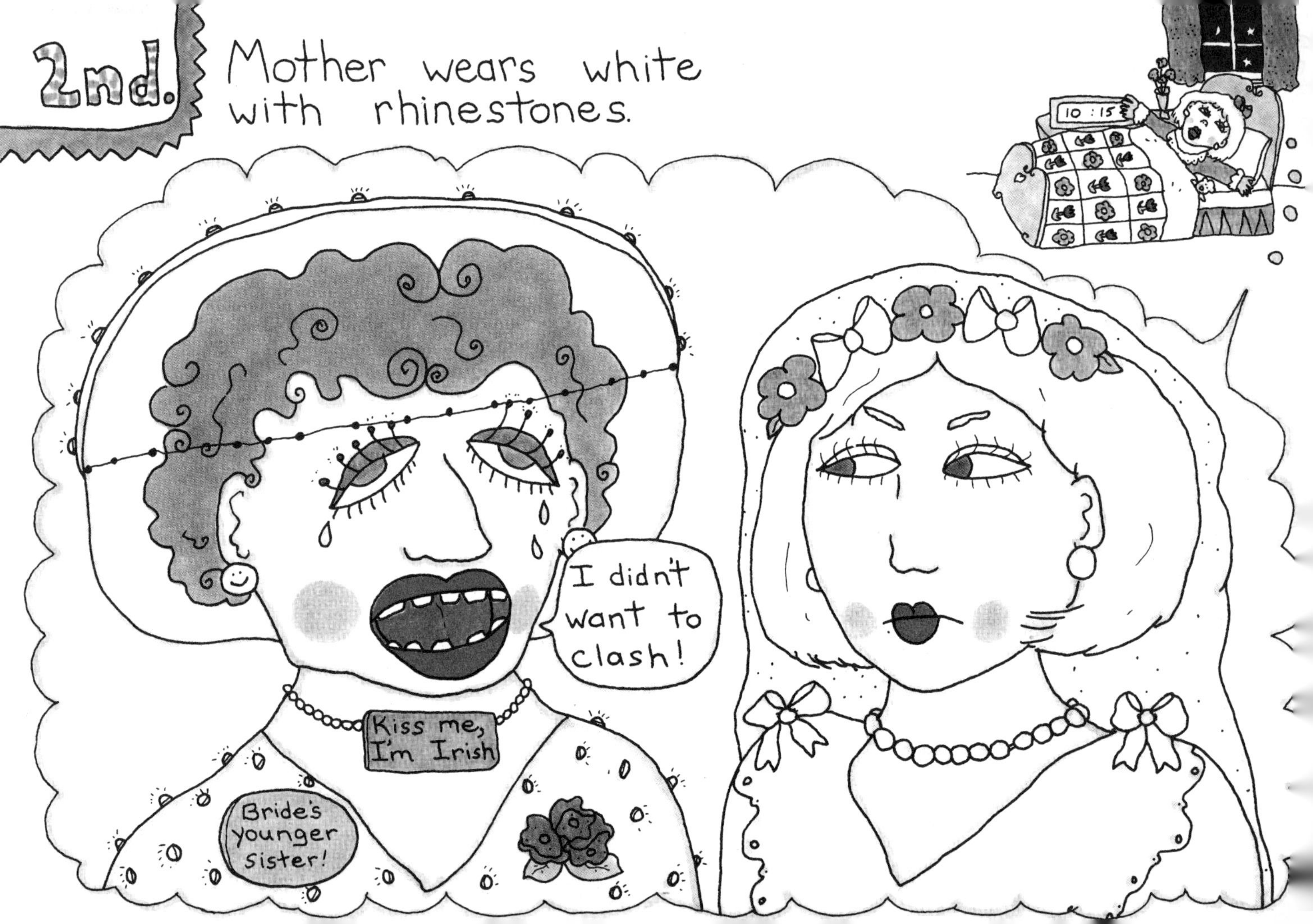
10 : 15
I didn't want to clash!
Kiss me, I'm Irish
Bride's younger sister!

3rd. Dad's toast is unsparingly detailed.

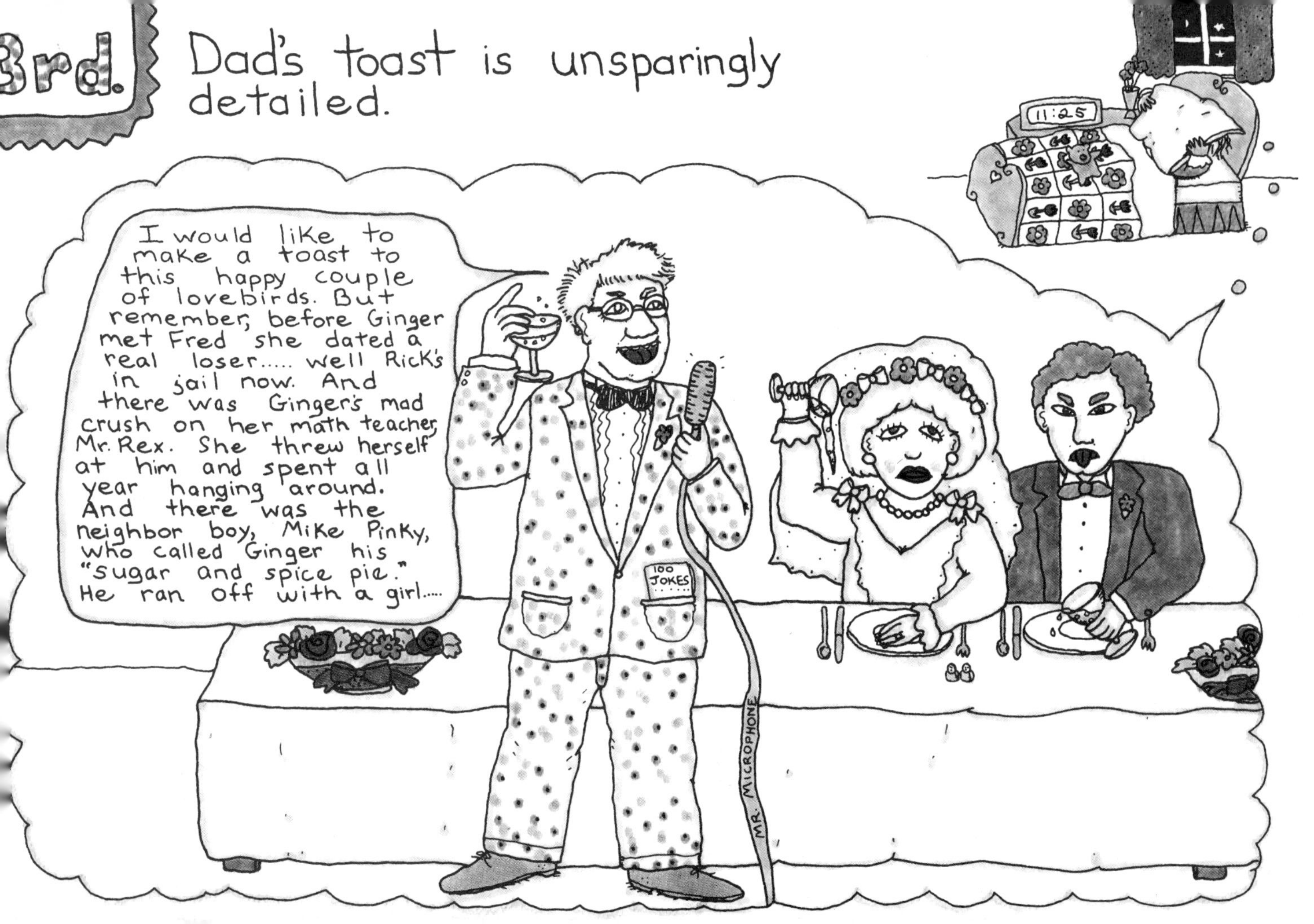
11:25
I would like to make a toast to this happy couple of lovebirds. But remember, before Ginger met Fred she dated a real loser..... well Rick's in jail now. And there was Ginger's mad crush on her math teacher, Mr. Rex. She threw herself at him and spent all year hanging around. And there was the neighbor boy, Mike Pinky, who called Ginger his "sugar and spice pie." He ran off with a girl.....
100 JOKES
MR. MICROPHONE

4th. Mother-in-law tells everyone what a happy occasion it is.

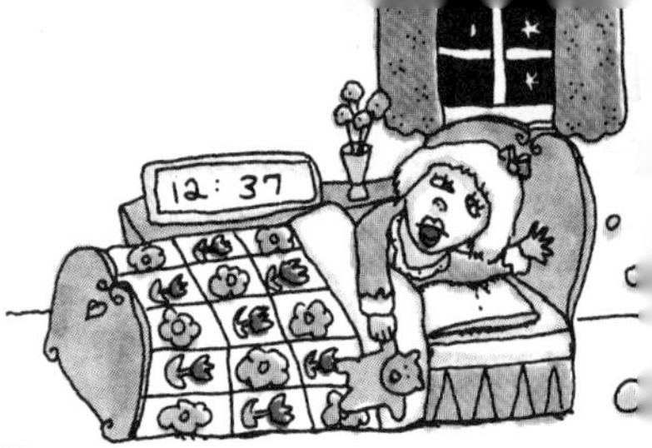
12:37

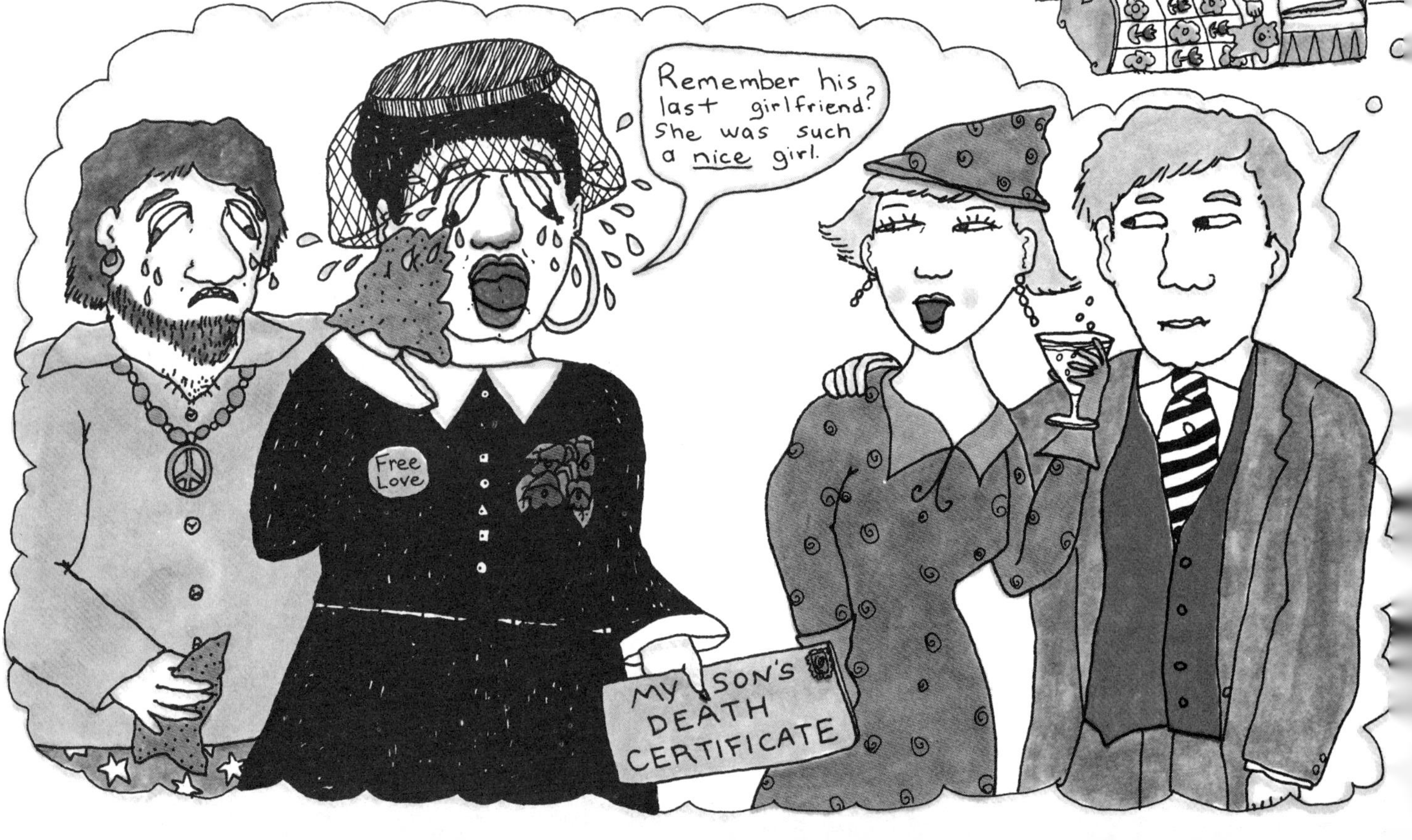
Remember his last girlfriend? She was such a nice girl.
Free Love
MY SON'S DEATH CERTIFICATE

5th. The groom disappears after his bachelor party.

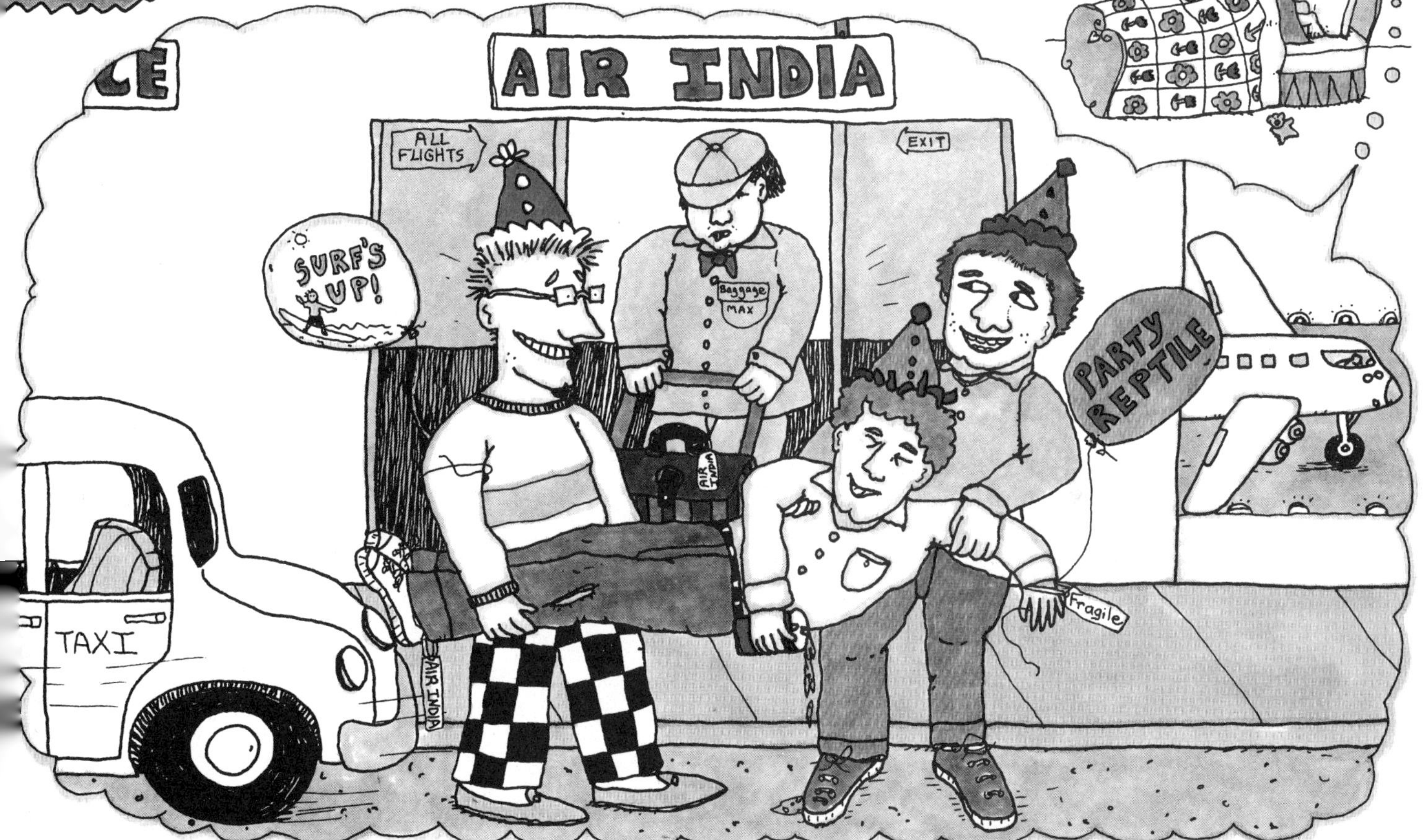

1:10
CE
AIR INDIA
ALL FLIGHTS
EXIT
SURF'S UP!
Baggage MAX
AIR INDIA
PARTY REPTILE
TAXI
AIR INDIA
Fragile

6th. The groom's old girlfriend appears out of the woodwork.

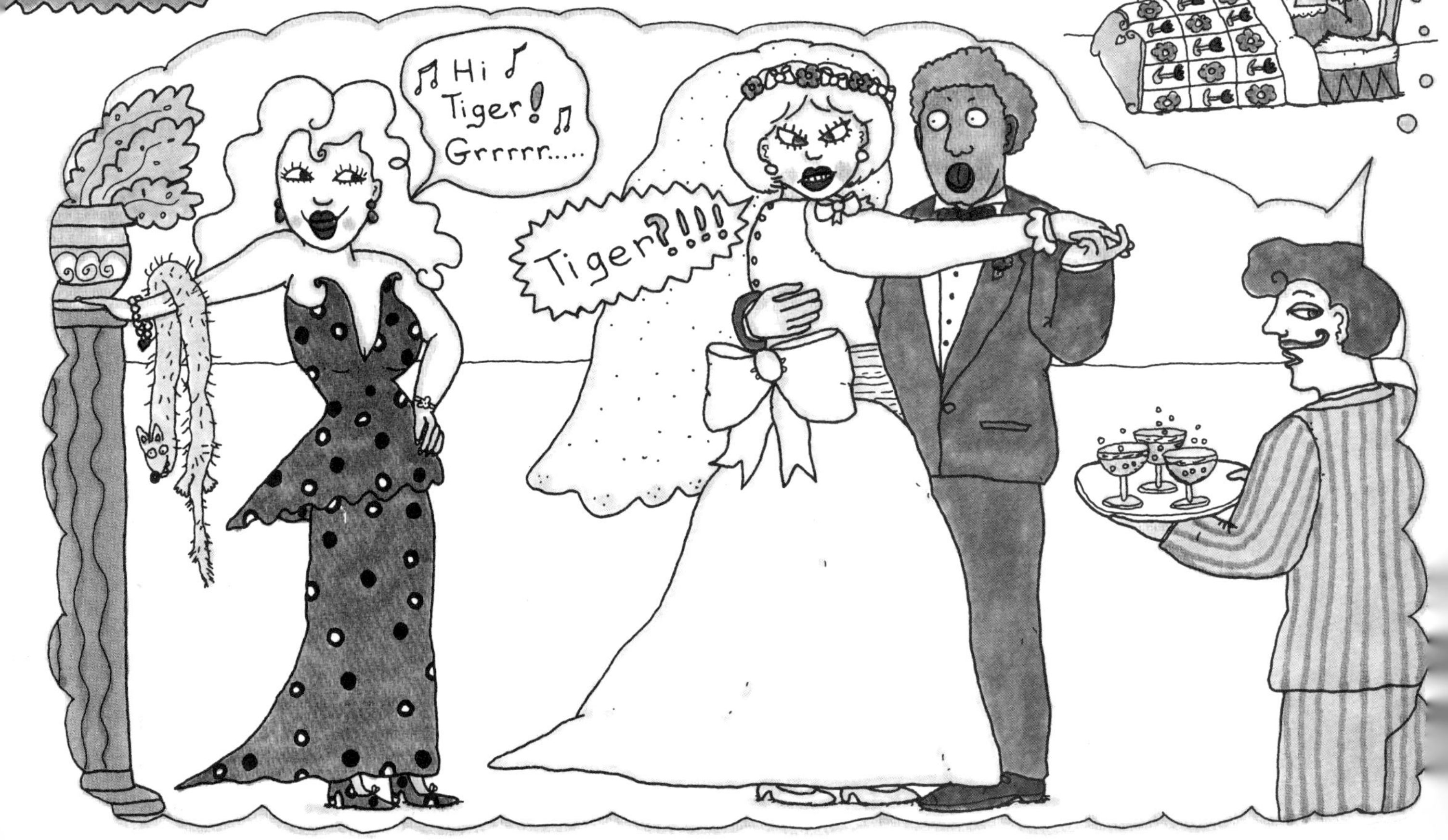
1:55
Hi Tiger! Grrrrr.....
Tiger?!!!!

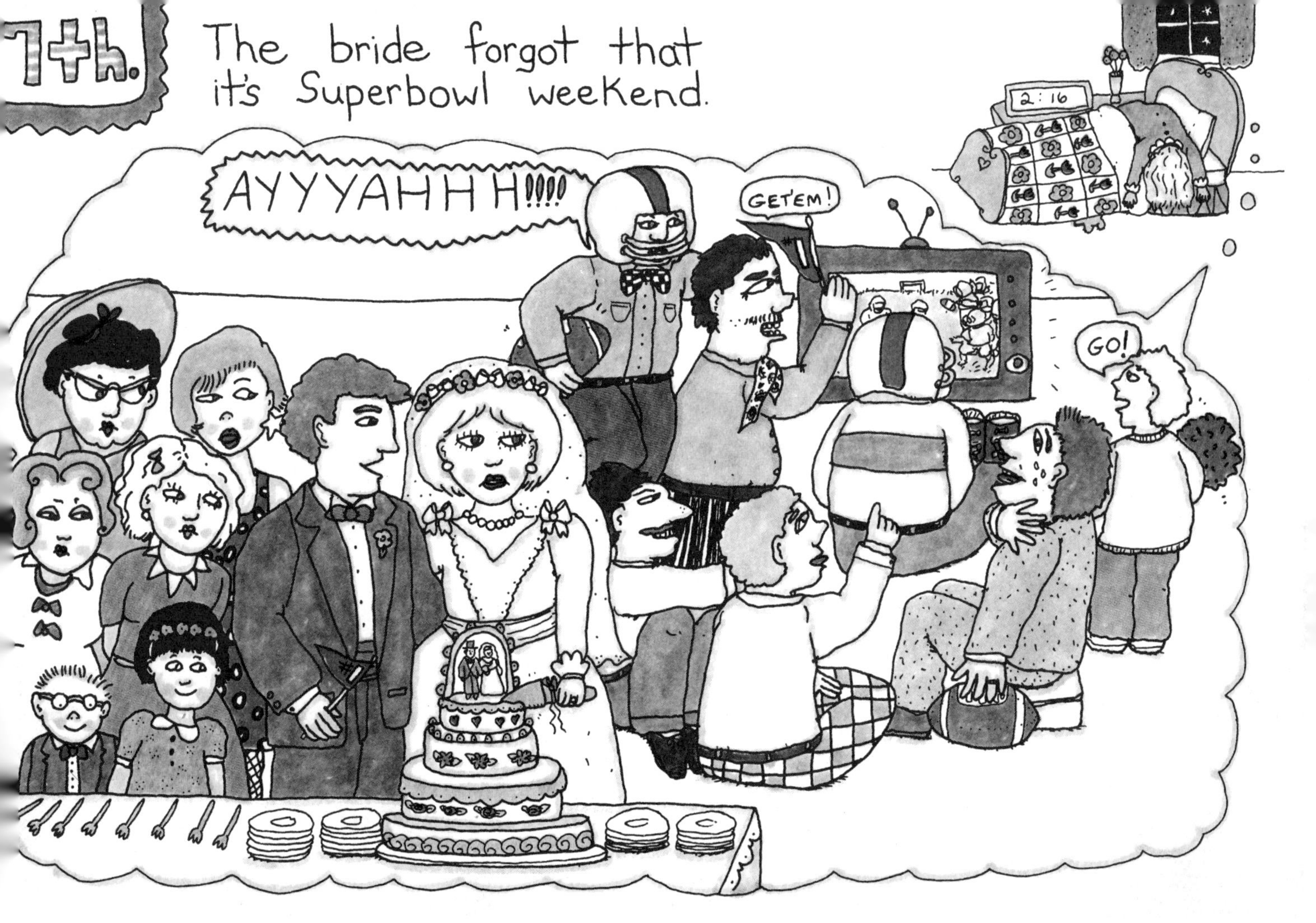
AYYYAHHH!!!!
GET'EM!
GO!
2:16

7th. The bride forgot that it's Superbowl weekend.

8th. A distant cousin arrives and gives birth in the aisle.

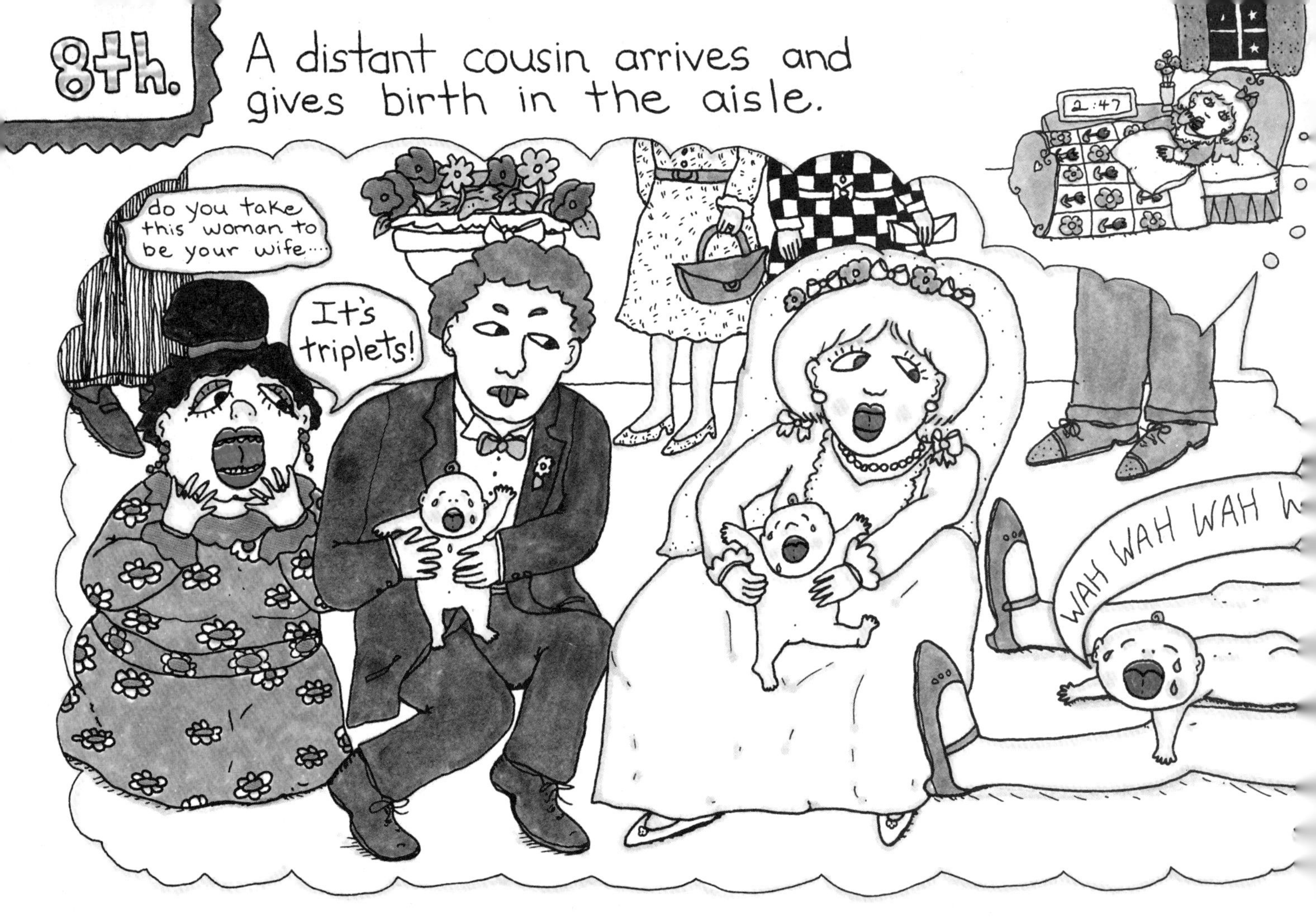
2:47
do you take this woman to be your wife....
It's triplets!
WAH WAH WAH W

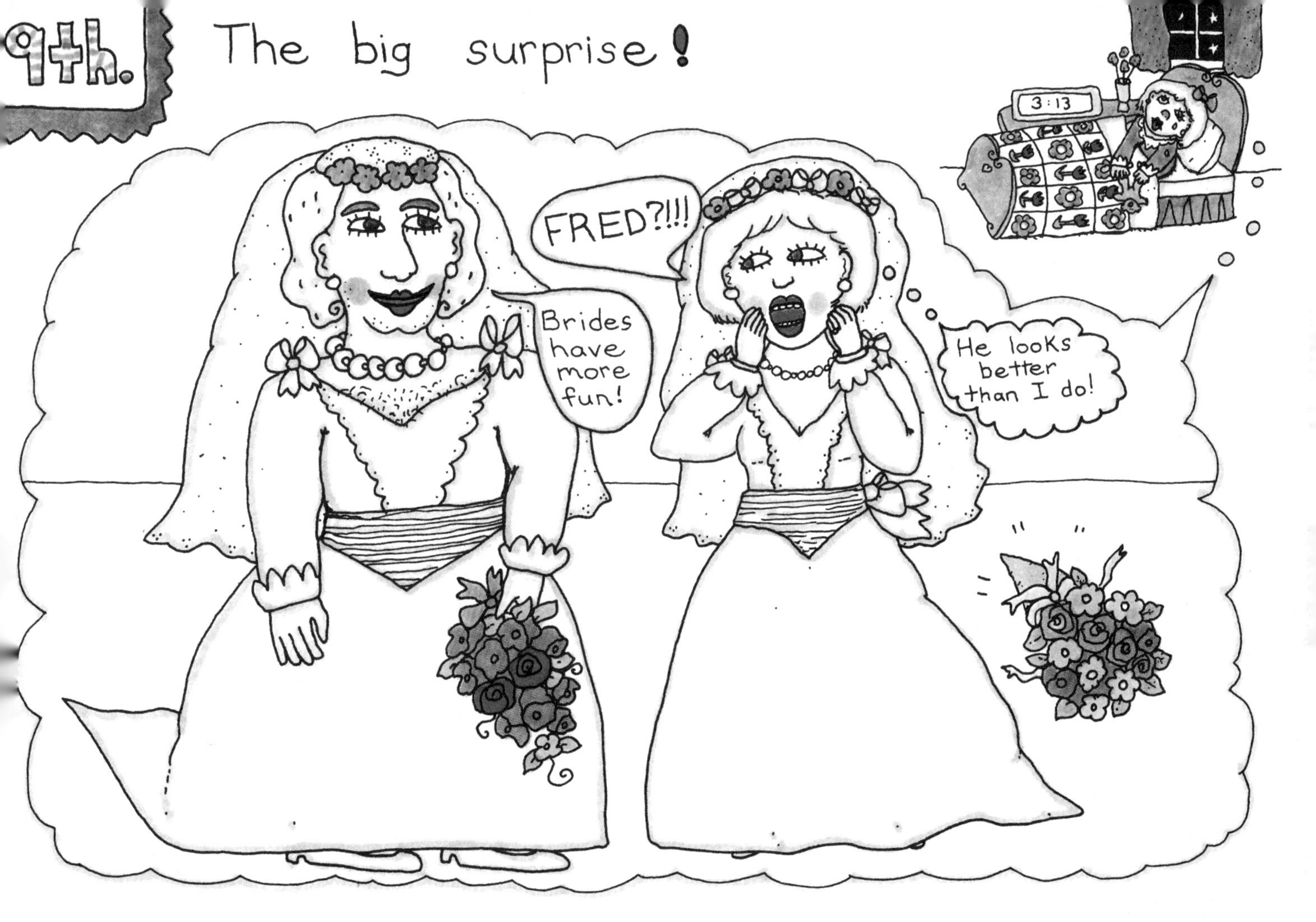
9th.
The big surprise!
3:13
FRED?!!!
Brides have more fun!
He looks better than I do!

10th. Death by rice.

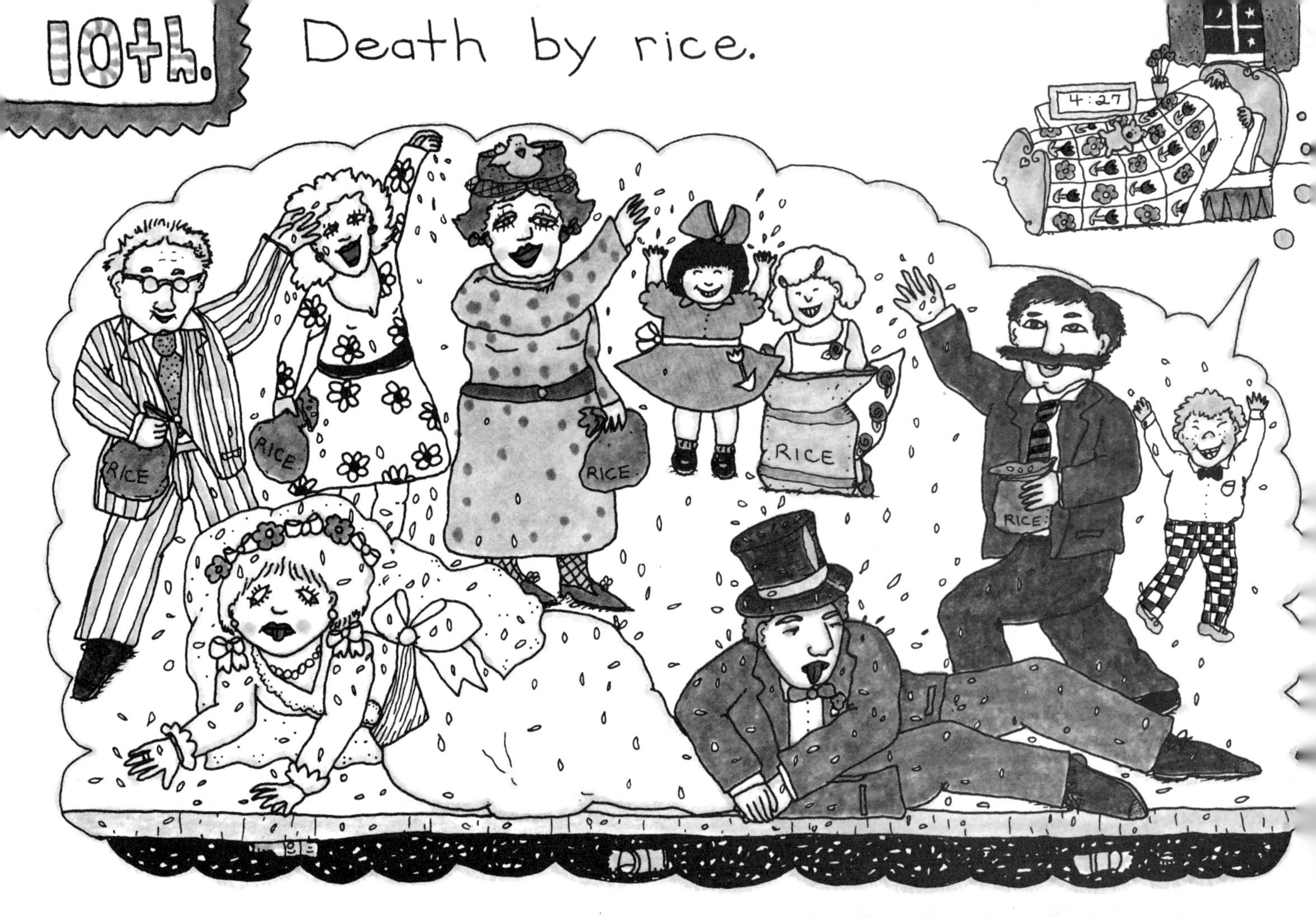
4:27
RICE
RICE
RICE
RICE
RICE

Remember, if you've followed our advice, everything will be just fine. Your wedding will be lovely, and the two of you can start your new life.

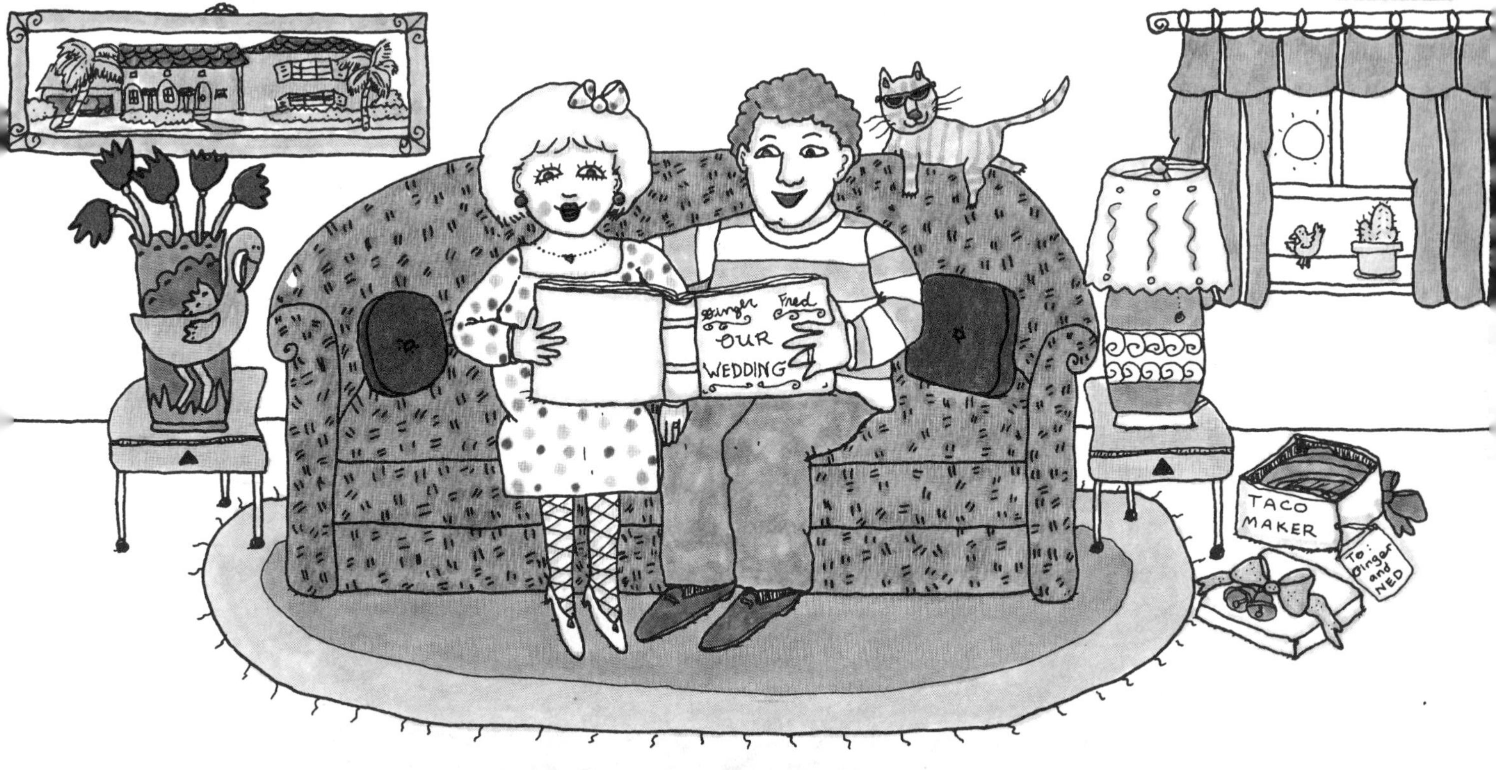

Fred
OUR
WEDDING
TACO
MAKER
To:
Ginger
and
NED

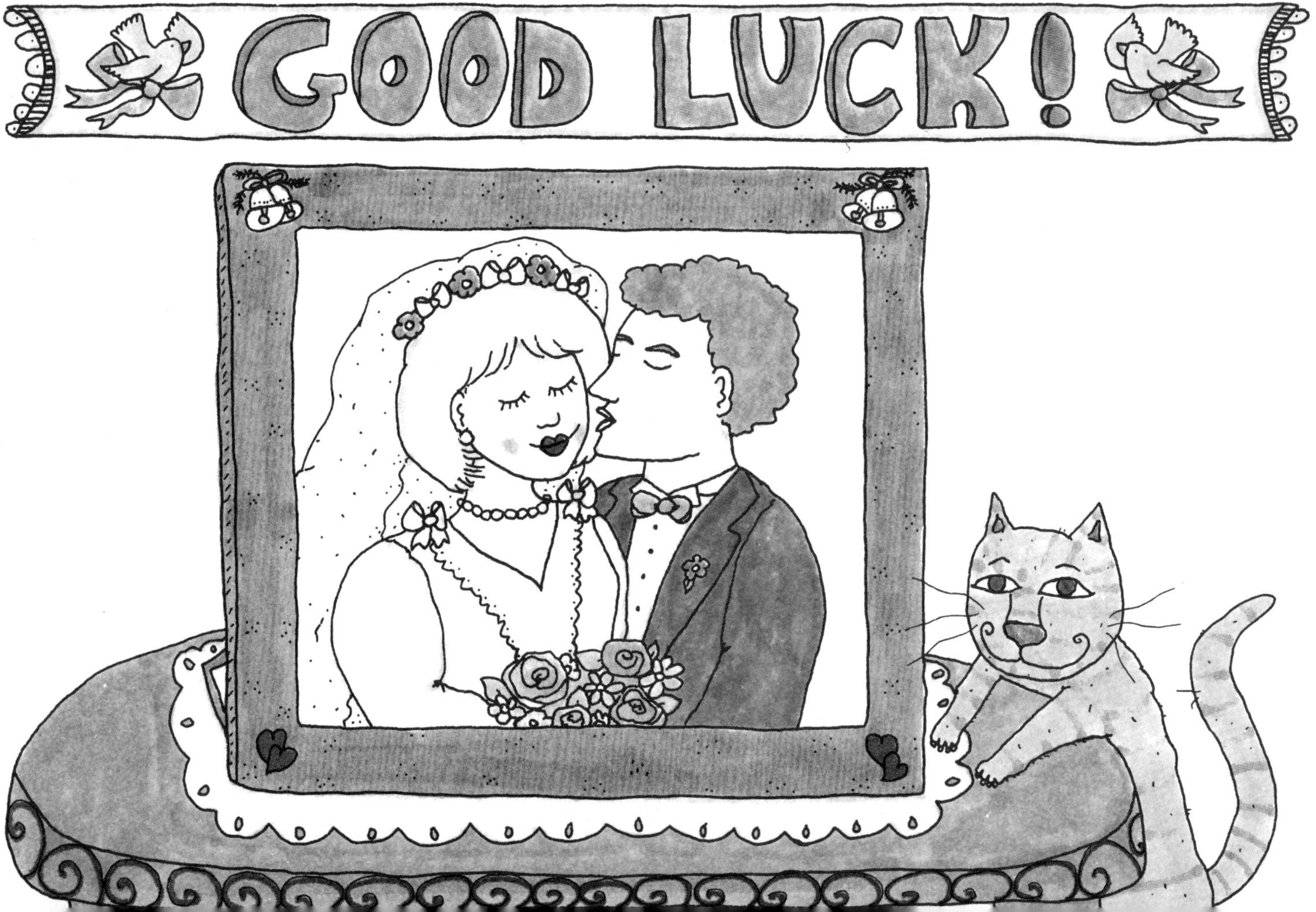
GOOD LUCK!